Stock Car Driving Techniques

WITH COMMENTARY BY JEFF GORDON, TERRY LABONTE, JEFF BURTON AND RICKY RUDD

Don Alexander
with special assistance from Bob Meyers

MBI Publishing Company

DEDICATION

To my wife, Christie, whose help and encouragement allows me to pursue endeavors that mean so much to me.

First published in 2001 by MBI Publishing Company, Galtier Plaza, Suite 200, 380 Jackson Street, St. Paul, MN 55101-3885, USA.

MBI Publishing Company books are also available at discounts in bulk quantity for industrial or sales-promotional use. For details write to Special Sales Manager at Motorbooks International Wholesalers & Distributors, Galtier Plaza, Suite 200, 380 Jackson Street, St. Paul, MN 55101-3885, USA.

Library of Congress Cataloging-in-Publication Data Available

ISBN:0-7603-0958-2

Edited by Paul Johnson
Designed by Jim Snyder

On the front cover: Jeff Gordon has a special talent for selecting the fastest lines and managing his tires; that's what makes the three-time Winston Cup champion so tough to beat. Gordon is arguably the most complete stock car driver today because he has developed fundamentals and continued building skills. *Nigel Kinrade*

On the frontispiece: Drivers and crew chiefs should have a symbiotic relationship. It's vitally important for the driver to effectively communicate the behavior of the car with the crew chief. A driver needs to develop a rapport and a common language with the crew chief, so the car's setup can be dialed-in to a particular track. *Nigel Kinrade*

On the title page: Jeff Gordon holds off Jimmy Hensley and Davey Allison in the 1993 Hanes 500. Gordon is able to hold the lead because he is monitoring and managing a number of different tasks at once—braking points, steering points, available traction, line selection, and the traffic behind. *Nigel Kinrade*

On the back cover: Dale Earnhardt won seven Winston Cup championships because he had the ability to efficiently manage on-track priorities and the many other facets of driving. He was able to concentrate on one particular task when necessary, and he could shift that focus to other areas. *Nigel Kinrade*

Printed in Hong Kong

CONTENTS

ACKNOWLEDGMENTS

Having participated in racing for over four decades, there are literally hundreds of people to thank. To all of them I want to express a heartfelt thank you. Without all the help, the journey would have ended long ago.

There are several people I want to thank for their specific help on this book. Most notably is Bob Myers who I worked with a Circle Track. Bob talked with the Winston Cup drivers to get their comments that have added so much to this work. And thanks also to Jeff Burton, Jeff Gordon, Terry Labonte and Ricky Rudd for taking time to provide invaluable commentary. Additional thanks to Mike and Krystal Loescher of the FinishLine Racing School. They run one of the best short track school programs in the country. Thanks to Arnie Kuhns from the SFI Foundation for his help and mostly for his hard work making sure that the safety equipment we all wear in race cars is the best and safest possible. Doug Stokes from Irwindale Speedway has helped with photo passes and more importantly, he's been helping me for over 33 years in this sport. Sheldon Tackett is my long-time crew chief. We have spent a long time trying to figure this stuff out and his help has been invaluable. And finally thanks to Paul Johnson from MBI Publishing. This project would have never happened without his hard work and guidance.

INTRODUCTION

Little in life equals the thrill of strapping into a stock car for a race on a short track. It's hard to believe that I first experienced that thrill over 25 years ago. And more surprising, the thrill of racing is just a great today as it was back then. In that time span, much has changed in the sport. Tires, shocks, race car dynamics and setup, safety equipment, costs, and popularity are worlds apart from a quarter-century ago. While the fundamentals of stock car race driving have remained the same, the driving styles have evolved. Much of that is reflected in the pages of *Stock Car Driving Techniques*.

I have raced, written about racing, and taught racing courses, so I have an intimate and unique perspective on the skills needed to be a competent, if not winning, race driver. I have taught those racing skills to others, to novice as well as experienced drivers attempting to go to the next level. The sum of that experience, knowledge, and perspective appears in these pages.

When I first started racing stock cars two and a half decades ago, driving skill and racecraft were the two most important ingredients for winning races. Safety was an afterthought for most of us, and race car dynamics were limited to tire stagger, wedge, and camber. Since 1976 chassis, suspension, and tire technology have grown by leaps and bounds. Today, race car dynamics and setup play an integral role in stock car racing. Therefore, a considerable portion of *Stock Car Driving Techniques* is devoted to race car dynamics, at least for the race driver. The driver who fails to understand the dynamics of the race car is lost, regardless of racecraft and driving skills. In today's racing world, a fast driver without an excellent setup is a mid-pack runner at best. A competent driver with a great setup can win, but a great driver with a mediocre setup has no chance.

In 2001, the stock car racer must have it all: solid driving skills, excellent racecraft skills, a solid working knowledge of race car dynamics and setup, and the best safety equipment available. Twenty-five years ago, most of us didn't realize all these components were essential for success. Today we do. And *Stock Car Driving Techniques* is an invaluable resource for the race driver to participate in one of the most exciting activities known to the human race. Enjoy!

ONE

Axioms of Racing

While every race driver has winning as an overall goal, winning is a difficult goal to achieve. Even with the skills, commitment, and desire to do whatever is necessary, each race has only one winner. Winning is an external goal, one that you have limited control over. There are too many factors beyond the driver's control that can interfere with your ability to win: luck, funding, and the competition are all factors that can make winning difficult.

There are two types of goals: external and internal. External goals, like winning races or championships, are goals that you have little control over, as we described above. The second type is the internal goal. Internal goals are goals you have complete control over. Car preparation, knowledge of race car dynamics, developing driving skills, using the best safety equipment, optimal physical conditioning, hunting for sponsors, and the manner in which you present yourself to the public are all factors you have nearly complete control over.

The distinction is simple with an example. Most of us need sponsorship to be able to race. Finding a sponsor is an external goal, since you may never contact the right company at the right time. But putting together a first class presentation and contacting 100 companies that may be good sponsorship prospects are things you have complete control over. And that is an internal goal, one you have total control of. By setting aside the external goals and focusing on the internal goals, you stand a better chance of reaching your external goals.

Winning more than 10 races in three years has made Tony Stewart one of Winston Cup's hottest commodities. Stewart demonstrates incredible car control skills as well as race craft. He has developed a solid winning strategy, but the controversial driver has been involved in a number of racing incidents. A driver must establish his or her race plan before strapping on the helmet. *Nigel Kinrade*

Johnny Benson is a Winston Cup driver who presents himself professionally, is physically fit, and has a positive attitude. Benson (on the far left) proudly stands with his crew before the start of the Brickyard 400. *Paul Johnson/Speed Sports Photography*

Your first internal goal is to become a successful stock car racer. You need to make a commitment to develop the skills necessary to win races. These include:

1. **Driving skills**
2. **Racecraft**
3. **Physical fitness**
4. **Race car dynamics and setup knowledge**
5. **Marketing skills**
6. **Public speaking skills**
7. **A positive physical image and personality**

It takes a lot of work to be successful in racing. These are essential long-term goals, and the driver with the best package typically is the most successful.

Here are other important elements of being a race driver that must be addressed.

SAFETY

Regardless of racing association rules, it is always the responsibility of the driver to drive a safe race car and use the best safety equipment. A commitment to safety can save your life, prevent injury, and lengthen your career. There is no legitimate reason to be slack about safety. A driver must understand the safety challenges and problems. A career-conscious driver will research the available equipment and use only the best. Most importantly, never drive a race car that you think is unsafe. To turn down a ride in a race car may be the most difficult decision you'll ever make, but your life depends on it.

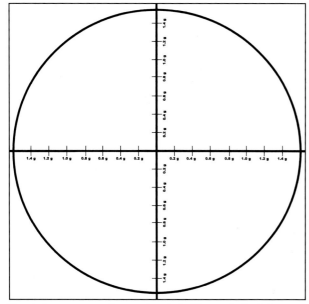

The circle represents the traction circle. The vertical axis is longitudinal acceleration, with braking from the center down and acceleration from the center up. The horizontal axis represents lateral cornering forces, with left turns from the center to the left and right turns from the center to the right. The farther along the axis, the higher the acceleration force.

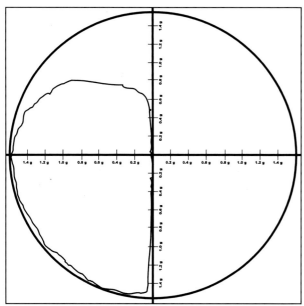

Force sensors in a race car generated the line inside the traction circle. It shows the car braking into a corner, turning left and then accelerating out of the corner. The entire segment seen here took about 10 seconds. This driver is using the tires very close to their limits of traction while braking and turning, then while turning and accelerating out of the corner. Even the most powerful race car cannot accelerate with the same force as it can decelerate or corner. Thus, the acceleration plot in the upper segment is lower.

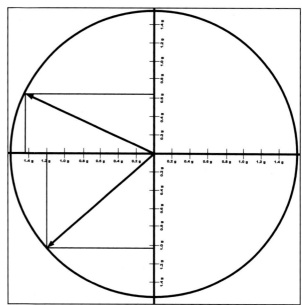

On this traction circle are two heavy arrows called vectors. Since the vector in each case is not directly on a vertical or horizontal axis, the vector line shows a force that is a combination of lateral and longitudinal forces. This means that some of the tire's traction is used for braking and cornering in the lower left quadrant. In the upper left segment, some of the tire's traction is being used for cornering and acceleration. In both cases, all of the tire's traction force is being used, because the vector line stops at the edge of the circle. The circle is used to represent the total maximum traction available for a given set of circumstances.

I know just how hard that is. I have also lost friends who chose to drive an unsafe car.

SPEED

Speed comes with practice and focusing on all of the things mentioned above. To go fast requires honest confidence, and honest confidence is earned through hard work. Cockiness, which many confuse with self-confidence, is an illusion, and will never take the place of paying your dues. The greatest drivers in the history of the sport allowed their race track performances to speak for their ability. When it comes time to find that last two- or three-tenths of a second, forget about time and focus on doing your job to perfection. A driver should slow down to execute every move perfectly. The speed will follow.

FINISHING

Being a successful race driver requires finishing races. Being harsh on equipment is quick path to a

The FinishLine Racing School

Why Go to a Racing School

If you are planning to race or have just started, a racing school will save you considerable time and money on the road to becoming an accomplished racer. First of all, in a multiple-day course, you will get several races' worth of experience. This will not be in a wheel-to-wheel racing situation, but will be experience that gets you up to speed much more quickly. With professional guidance, you will learn at a faster rate. Typically, a two-or three-day school is worth about a season of racing experience. Additionally, the seat time and professional training can save you from making costly mistakes that put you into the wall.

Reasonable Expectations

If you are thinking about going to a racing school, you should have some idea about what you want to achieve at the school, but also be clear about what the school can actually offer you. Over the years, I've had students who expected much more than a school could ever deliver. In a seven-hour day at the track, you cannot expect to spend all of that time in a car. Race cars are very expensive capital expenditures for the school operator. Expect to share a car with several other students. Racing is also dangerous. Most crashes occur when race cars collide with each other. Schools often have only one car on the track at a time.

FinishLine Racing School

I've trained thousands of race drivers over the years as an instructor at several schools. I've also attended the FinishLine School in Florida. For someone wanting to learn how to race stock cars, there is not a better program available. They do it right from safety, to cars, to on-track instruction. I am not aware of another school that provides the level of instruction and the quality program available from Mike and Kristal Loescher, operators of the Finish-Line Racing School.

As chief instructor of the school, Mike Loescher brings more than 30 years of success and championship racing to the Finish-Line Racing School. Mike is a former NASCAR modified driver from upstate New York. He started racing at the age of 16, and continued to race professionally for 15 years before moving to Florida. Mike has had an impressive racing career. He has been credited with seven track championships and has over 130 victories to his name.

Mike has a unique ability to watch a race car and determine if it's the driver making a mistake or the race car. Not only is Mike a champion-caliber race car driver, he is also a chassis expert. And that's why the FinishLine Racing School works so well. Without a combination of chassis and driving knowledge, how can a driving coach help you? They can't. That's why Mike is the best.

Each day Mike walks the track with the students. This serves two purposes. First they look for debris that could cut a tire. Second, Mike points out different elevation changes in the asphalt that will seem to make the car respond differently. Without this knowledge, a driver could miscalculate and have the crew make a chassis change that the race car really didn't need. To race and win you have to understand everything—the race car, the race track, and your own driving style.

Kristal Loescher has been involved in racing for many years. She started out as the crew chief on Mike's "all-girl pit crew." Up until November 1987, Kristal had never raced in actual modified competition. As the school's first student, Kristal's first year was an impressive one. Of the 73 races she entered, she had 6 feature wins, 52 top five finishes, 13 heat race wins, and was second in the modified point championship.

The rapid success in her racing career was a direct result of Mike's coaching. It was at this point that Mike realized that he had a unique talent to share with the racing public that was hungry for knowledge.

Kristal's main objective in the school is to record the students' lap times and write down comments to be used by Mike as he's debriefing the student. The notes are constructive criticism and meant to point out a student's driving "weaknesses." The time sheets are passed out to each student at the end of each day.

The cars used at FinishLine meet NASCAR competition Late Model, NASCAR All Pro, Late Model Stock Truck, Sportsman, Grand American "Open Wheel" Modified and Super Truck specifications. The Finish-Line Racing School is a first class opera-tion. Safety is the primary concern. You will start the class with a full safety presentation, including video and graphic illustrations of the latest advances in fire-suits, helmets and in-car safety products. You will see an illustration of the effec-tiveness of the Nomex multi-layer firesuit. You will learn about the way seat belts and helmets are designed to absorb ener-gy in collisions. Students wear full Nomex firesuits and safety protection while rac-ing. All race cars are up-to-date racing machines and have on-board fire extin-guishers. Students' safety is paramount in all the driving exercises.

Some schools offer only racing adventures geared toward the race fan and corporate

The author has used his considerable experience to teach the principles of race driving to others. This school uses race trucks for driver training.

individuals, which FinishLine also provides. But FinishLine is more geared to the beginning racer or the racer who is already driving and having problems getting to the checkered flag. They teach strategy, chassis changes, driving style, and smoothness, all the elements to race "smart." When comparing different race schools, ask questions. Don't just go with "famous" names labeled on race schools—make sure you know what your tuition includes. If you will be competing at a Saturday night short track, you should attend a "short track" racing school. If you're racing "grass roots" why would you attend a "superspeedway" school? In addition to standard classes, FinishLine offers private race classes, one student/two race cars. With another race car on the track, you work on passing and traffic maneuvers. Mike also is available for private coaching where he works with you, your race car, and your crew at your race track.

FinishLine Racing Courses

FinishLine Racing School "Competition Driving Course" *(2 days, est. laps 86)*

Short track racing is where every past or current NASCAR, Indy, ARCA, IMCA, and ASA driver started. Short track racing skills are something not to be left behind once a driver enters the top professional auto racing series. The ratio of students to instructors at the FinishLine Racing School is three to one, giving you the individual attention you need. Students are in constant radio communication with their instructors, allowing race school instructors to correct mistakes as they happen, and to give advice and encouragement at every turn. The bottom line is that each student gets maximum seat time, each lap is logged, and students can achieve faster speeds each time out.

You'll Learn More in Three Days Than You Will on Your Own in Three Years!
(3 days, est. laps 138)

This three-day race school course is designed to give the first-time driver full exposure to short track racing. It also provides the experienced racer who has not yet reached victory circle the professional skills needed to go fast and take the checkered flag. Following the Competition Driving Course, you will further refine your skills and driving ability learned in the Late Model stock car. You will also have the chance to move into a NASCAR Grand American Modified. An added attraction to the three-day course is the chance to drive a Super Truck!

DNF (did not finish) or poor finishing position. Overdriving is slower driving. It abuses tires, chassis, suspension, and often everything else on the car. In addition, it often leads to a quick trip into the fence. Neither allows for success.

WINNING

Winning races is the result of developing solid-to-superior driving skills, finding a good setup, being patient, and developing genuine self-confidence.

INTEGRITY

Integrity is a personal choice for each of us. Winning by intentionally taking out other drivers lacks integrity, and I believe it creates a very hollow victory. You won't be held in high esteem among your peers, and questionable driving incidents most likely will be repaid in turn. In addition, hard racing can lead to racing incidents, and there is a very fine line between hard racing and a lack of integrity. It is important to establish an ethical standard of driving conduct before a race, because

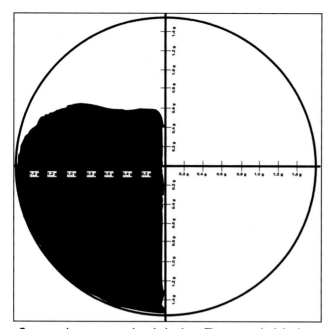 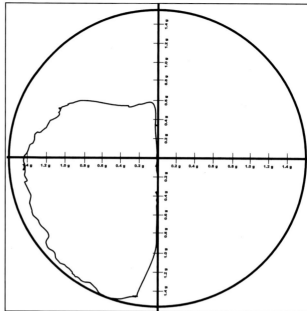

Compare these two traction circle plots. The one on the left shows a driver using much more of the tire's available traction than the driver on the right. Additionally, the driver on the right is using the controls more abruptly, and this reduces speed. While far from perfect, the driver on the left will get through the segment covered in this plot much faster than the driver on the right.

you'll be unable to make a distinction with clarity in the heat of battle.

CHEATING

Cheating, simply stated, is knowingly breaking the rules. Each of us must walk a fine line between "being legal" and cheating. But one must consider what the rules are. Are the rules what is written in a book, or are the rules what the officials actually enforce? Most racers define rules as what is being enforced.

RACE CAR DYNAMICS

The most important knowledge you can possess is a strong understanding of race car dynamics. That is as important as driving skills in stock car racing.

DRIVING SKILLS AND RACECRAFT

While driving skills are extremely important, being the fastest driver on the track is not the most important factor to success in racing. Racecraft—the ability to handle traffic, passing, defending position, tire management, race starts and restarts—is the most important factor in racing success. Dale Earnhardt was rarely the fastest driver, but his superior racecraft and driving skills often led him to victory lane or a top five finish.

THE TRACTION CIRCLE THEORY

Tires aren't smart. Tires don't know if they're turning, braking, or accelerating, so they are perfectly willing to brake and corner or accelerate and corner at the same time. The fact that tires can do this dictates the parameters in which a race car can be driven.

If you studied physics in high school (if you had only realized that physics class was really about race cars), you may remember a topic called vector analysis. A vector is an arrow that is used to represent a force. The length of the arrow represents the amount of force and where it points represents the direction of the force. A vector can be broken into two perpendicular elements to show the force acting along different planes. Or conversely, the vector arrow is the result of forces acting on two planes. For our purposes, the traction circle diagram indicates the maximum amount of traction available from the tires on a race car. The vector arrow shows the direction of the force and how close the traction force comes to the maximum available traction. We can analyze the vector by breaking it into its forces along the lateral force axis and the longitudinal force axis. We can see how much cornering force is available versus the amount of longitudinal force (braking

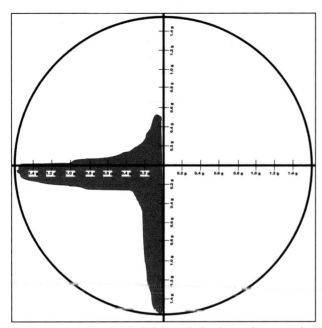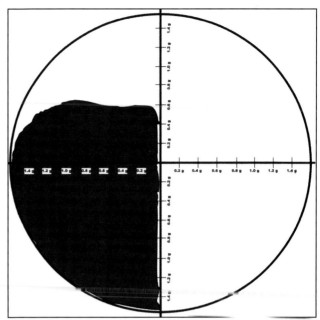

In this traction plot, the shaded areas depict the total amount of traction force used through this segment from the braking zone on the straight to the exit of the corner to the next braking zone. The shaded plot on the right has much more area than the one on the left. This means the driver on the right has used much more traction. In fact, nearly all of the available traction from the tires has been used. The driver on the right has used very little. The driver on the left has done all the braking in a straight line, released the brakes before turning, made it all the way through the corner without accelerating, and only began to accelerate when the steering wheel was turned straight at the exit of the corner. It's easy to see why the driver on the right is considerably faster than the one on the left. That's why the traction circle theory is so important.

or acceleration). If the vector angle is at 45 degrees from the vertical (or horizontal), half of the tires' traction is used for cornering and the other half is used for braking or acceleration. But if we carefully measure the lateral and longitudinal elements of the vector, we find that the length of each is 70.7 percent of the total. This means we are able to do more work by staying as close to the edge of the traction circle as possible. If we do not do this, precious time is lost around the race track. Study the traction circle diagrams and explanations carefully in this section so that you fully understand this crucial concept.

FINDING THE LIMIT

One of the most crucial skills of a race driver is finding the limits of traction without exceeding, or overdriving, those limits. After studying the traction circle diagrams, you realize how important driving at the limits of traction is to fast lap times. Anything short of the traction circle edge costs valuable time. Overdriving reduces traction,

produces excessive wear on the car's components, and again costs valuable time. So how do you find the sweet spot?

Unfortunately, there is no buzzer blaring or light flashing in the driver's compartment as you approach the limit of traction. An acute sense of feel is needed to sense the traction limit. The top professional drivers (Jeff Gordon, Terry Labonte, Mark Martin, and many others) have developed a fine feel for available traction. You use the seat of your pants, hands, feet, and sense of balance to sense traction. It takes some natural ability, but mostly it takes track time to develop the senses to a high degree. It is crucial to develop these skills.

A driver needs to begin by learning the feel of the limit under braking, then acceleration, and finally cornering. Practice each separately and build a solid foundation before integrating the skills. Build up force gradually for each of the three skills, sensing the traction and forces as you use more traction. With practice, you will begin to sense the limit, and you will recognize when you start to exceed the limit of the brakes, throttle, or steering. Once you have developed a solid feel for each individual control, integrate cornering with braking, and acceleration with cornering. Try different paths while doing this, so that you can feel the relationship between the steering and braking forces, and the acceleration and steering forces. Refer to Chapter 2 (Using the Controls) for more information.

TRACTION SAMPLING

While learning to find the limit, you were sampling traction—it's pretty much automatic. You can develop your ability to sample traction by focusing more attention on the forces acting on you and the car. By paying greater attention to how the car feels, you will develop more sensitivity to traction and lateral/longitudinal forces. The more you develop this skill, the more attention you will have available to work on racecraft.

UNDERSTEER AND OVERSTEER

If you've ever watched a stock car race on TV, you've heard the terms "push" and "loose." Push is understeer, which means the front tires lose traction before the rear tires. When a car understeers or pushes, it is referred to as being "tight." On the other end of the spectrum, when a car oversteers, it is referred to as being "free" or "loose." The rear tires lose traction before the front tires. The front tires slide toward the wall with understeer and the rear tires slide toward the wall with oversteer. When both front and rear tires slide equally, the car is neutral. A race car's handling balance (oversteer-neutral-understeer) is determined by the setup of the car and when and how the driver uses the controls.

THE MENTAL APPROACH

While physical fitness, car control, and race car dynamics are all very important, driving a race car is a mental game. The best mentally prepared driver has the best chance to win. Each of these elements is explored in greater detail in the following chapters. Take your time and enjoy the journey.

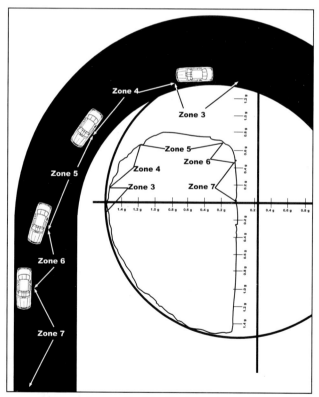

These two diagrams show traction circle plots with a car position diagram overlaid for reference. The left side shows the middle of a turn to the exit onto the straight. The right side diagram shows braking onto the straight and turning into the corner. It is most important to note that the combinations of braking and steering and steering and throttle application must be perfectly balanced at each point in the corner to keep the car on the edge of the traction circle and use all of the available tire traction.

TWO

Using the Controls

Developing solid control-use skills is the first order of business for any new driver. If a driver doesn't have a good grasp of the fundamentals, a driver will not able to turn competitive lap times. In turn, he or she will find it virtually impossible to improve skills.

After winning several races, the car owner has to change drivers for this race. The new driver is very experienced, having won races in your division at this track. The car is set up exactly the same with identical crossweights and weight percentages, stagger, and other settings. The car was well balanced with the original driver. The new driver goes out for the first practice session and comes in complaining of a big push. You confirm this visually and the front tire temperatures are very high, with the average front temps over 40 degrees hotter than the rear averages. You increase stagger, and the lap times are faster, but the push is almost as bad. Next you reduce wedge, but the car still has a big push. What's going on here?

THE TRACTION CIRCLE

The traction circle theory states that tire traction can be used for cornering, acceleration in a straight line, or braking in a straight line. Traction can also be used for a combination of cornering and braking or cornering and acceleration. In fact, if the driver does not use the tire's traction for these combinations, the total traction available is not being completely utilized, and speed is

The 1999 Winston Cup Champion Dale Jarrett is able to keep his car on the threshold of traction for extended periods of time. Often times, it is the difference between winning and being an also ran. Remember, winning often comes down to sensing the amount of available traction in the tires and extracting the best performance from those tires over a long period time. *Nigel Kinrade*

lost around the race track. On the other hand, the driver cannot go faster than the available traction allows. And any effort the driver makes to exceed this limit of traction will *slow* the car.

The basic problem occurs when the driver applies too much steering wheel lock for the amount of brake force or acceleration being used. A driver's abrupt use of the controls can make the situation even worse. Jerky, sudden steering wheel movements, stabbing the brake pedal suddenly or burying your foot on the throttle pedal not only can make the traction situation worse, but can cause the problem as well. Look at the accompanying graphs and charts to see what occurs.

For any given situation, there is only one optimum combination of steering wheel lock and brake pedal force or throttle pedal application. For instance, all traction can be used for braking with no steering application; the same applies with acceleration in a straight line. Or all traction can be used for cornering without acceleration or deceleration. When two activities are combined, the driver is walking a two-dimensional tightrope in the effort to stay on the edge of the traction circle. Underdriving or overdriving will cost time and speed around the race track. The driver must constantly seek and maintain a line as close to the perfect balance as his or her ability allows. This is the key to being a fast race driver and is exactly why driving a race car at the limits of traction is an art form.

Two factors apply—the amount and rate of control. First is the amount the control is used, which directly correlates to the traction circle. The second factor is the rate at which the control is used. When it comes to brake and throttle application, the pedals should be squeezed on, like pulling the trigger on a gun. The release of the pedals should be progressive and gentle, not abrupt. The steering wheel should be turned as slowly as possible to keep the car on the desired path. Abrupt steering can induce a push or loose situation. And if this is combined with abrupt pedal use, the dynamics can disturb the balance of the car and cause a trip into the wall.

A driver can take a well-handling car and cause it to be loose or to push, depending on what is done with the controls. A driver can also take an ill-handling car and improve the situation by using care with the controls. Let's look more closely at the techniques and skills needed to use the controls.

> When you first apply the throttle pedal, you do it easy, not hard at all. It's a very gentle motion, especially when the tires get worn. In qualifying with fresh tires, you can use the throttle harder. You have to drive the car to the limits of the tires. The way you drive the car can change how long before the tires actually start slippin' and slidin' around. Good tire management is a lot more critical at some tracks than others. Generally, the flatter the race track, the more you have to take care of the tires. The biggest thing is when you drive the car you can feel the edge of the tire. If you exceed that edge, and exceed it very aggressively, you end up sliding the tire across the race track. That builds more heat, which builds more pressure, so that compounds the problem. You have to learn how to run the car right on the edge of wheelspin and not go beyond that.
>
> *–Jeff Gordon*

EFFECTIVE BRAKING TECHNIQUES

It is helpful to look at the reason brakes are used in a race car. The last thing you want to do is slow the car, because the goal is to go as fast as possible around the race track. Braking is counter to this. But to stay on the race track and out of the fence, you must slow the car to negotiate the turns. But you want to slow the car as little as necessary to maintain maximum speed through the turns. Slow too much, and you lose time; slow too little, and the car slides, scrubbing off speed, and you lose time. The goal is to slow the exact amount necessary in the shortest time possible. This braking technique will get you around the race track as quickly as possible, and this brings us to a basic law of racing: The driver on full throttle for the longest period of time will be the fastest, all else being equal. Additionally, this leads to a corollary of this law: The driver who slows the least will be fastest.

BRAKING PRINCIPLES AND THE LAWS OF PHYSICS

Like any part of racing, braking must follow the laws of physics. Let's look at those laws and how they affect the way you drive a race car.

Braking occurs without applying the brakes. Applying the brakes is not the only way to decelerate a car. Releasing the throttle will also cause a car to decelerate. It still takes traction from the tires to decelerate this way. The braking force comes through the engine and driveline instead of the brake calipers and rotors, but it still takes traction force from the tires to slow the car.

Braking performance is reduced by wheel lockup. When a single wheel locks up under braking, traction is reduced at that wheel. If all four wheels lock while braking, traction is lost at all four corners. A sliding tire makes less traction than a rolling tire. Maximum traction occurs well before wheel lockup occurs. If a single wheel locks up before the others, overall traction while decelerating is reduced from optimum. It is important to have the brake system well set up and for the driver to develop braking skills and sensitivity to a high level. Little time can be gained underbraking, but considerable time can be lost.

Braking performance and handling are hindered when the throttle is not completely released. This may sound basic, but happens so often that it is truly a problem. It overheats the brakes, affects weight transfer, increases the distance needed for slowing, and wears the brakes unmercifully. The problem is usually caused by the throttle pedal position relative to the driver's foot. This occurs only when a driver brakes with his left foot. Be aware of this as a potential problem, check pedal placement, and make sure to pull the right foot completely away from the throttle pedal as you apply the brakes.

Tire traction is proportional to the vertical load on the tire. Tire traction increases as vertical load increases on a given tire. Traction also decreases as vertical load decreases. When weight transfers during braking, the vertical loads are constantly changing on the tire. Therefore the traction on each tire changes. This changing traction affects overall vehicle traction as well as the front-to-rear handling balance of the car.

Tires realize maximum traction under braking with a small amount of slipping. Under braking, maximum traction occurs at about 10 percent slippage, meaning that the tire is actually locked up for 10 out of 100 feet of stopping distance. Or more accurately, 1/10 inch for every inch traveled while limit braking.

Super late braking is not effective. On paper, waiting until the last possible instant to apply the brakes, then braking at the limit of traction until speed is reduced to the correct amount to negotiate the corner seems like the fastest method. It is on paper, but not on the race track.

Braking at the last instant, then braking at the limit of traction makes it difficult to get the car through the middle of the turn and off the corner as fast as possible. If fast lap times are the goal, getting off the corners is more important than getting into the corners. Without exception, a small sacrifice in corner-entry braking translates into saved time at the exit.

Ask yourself this question. "How much time do I spend braking at my race track?" The answer should be a very small percentage of the overall lap time. Therefore, braking is less important than acceleration out of the corners.

Let's use one of the toughest tracks ever for braking (the defunct Saugus Speedway) as an example. Saugus is a billiard table-like flat third-mile oval with long straights and tight corners. Braking is critical at Saugus compared to many other tracks. A competitive Street Stock laps Saugus in about 19 seconds. The time actually spent on the brakes in each corner is about 1.5 seconds, or about 3 seconds a lap. That's only 16 percent of a lap. About 13 to 14 seconds a lap is spent accelerating. That's about 76 percent of the total lap. The more time on the gas, the faster the speeds and the lap times. Thus, we want to minimize time on the brakes and maximize time on the throttle. So far, it seems that the late, hard-braking routine is the hot ticket. But this is only on paper. There is a trade-off here. Spending less time on the brakes also translates into spending less time on the throttle. Hence, lap times suffer. Sacrifice a little speed into the turn, and get a better, quicker, and harder exit from the turn. Do this lap after lap, and tires will work better for longer periods, and brakes will also last longer. Hard, but not drastic, braking will allow you to rotate the car more easily in mid-turn and allow a better line for peak acceleration off the corner. By sacrificing about 1 second of braking time entering the corner, you save time over the 7 seconds at the exit. You can save a lot more time over the 7 seconds than you can over the 1/10-second period going in.

Even if you could have the best of both worlds, which you can't, the very tiny time savings entering the corner (less than 0.1 second) isn't worth the risk of losing time at the exit. Execution under braking has to be perfect for every turn, lap after lap.

The demand of braking on your attention is an additional consideration. As you begin braking into the corner, you need to switch attention from entering the corner under brakes to exiting the corner under peak acceleration. Absolute limit braking takes 100 percent of your concentration at a time you cannot afford to focus 100 percent on braking. If all you had to do to win was be first into the corner and then stop, we would have a different set of priorities, but I've never seen a race won entering a turn. The finish line is just past the exit.

Another factor is changing traction conditions. Traction rarely improves during a race, but it could. Braking is the first place you can notice changing traction. If you're at the absolute limit while braking, you cannot make an adjustment going into the corner if traction has been reduced. By braking just below the limit, you have some room for adjustment.

So how much less do you brake going in? I've never had a chance to measure it, but it's in the range of 85 to 95 percent of the maximum braking capacity. That slight reduction to braking costs very little time, but saves a bundle when it comes time to get down the next straightaway.

One of the most difficult aspects of stock car racing is taking positions under braking. The shorter the track, and the less braking required, the more difficult the pass becomes. But one of the keys to passing is using effective braking techniques. Additionally, effective braking technique will allow faster laps. If there is one aspect of race car driving that is misused, it is braking.

MANAGING WEIGHT TRANSFER DURING BRAKING

To achieve maximum braking performance, brake bias must be perfect and the vertical load from left to right must be equal. Otherwise, one or more wheels could lock prematurely, reducing braking performance. In the vast majority of cases, the left front is the first to lock up on a stock car on an oval. Here's why. Most stock cars have about 56 percent left-side static weight. About 10 percent of the weight will transfer from the left to the right in a turn. Most of this transfer is at the front.

The rear ends up nearly equal in weight, but the left front is somewhat lighter than the right front, especially with a lot of crossweight in the car. The light load on the left front, combined with equal pressure on the brake pads on the front brakes, means the left front will lock up first on most cars (assuming the front-to-rear bias is correct). This can cause a push do to the lightly loaded left front and the stressed right front tire contact patch.

> **I apply the brake pedal fairly aggressively without upsetting the car, using a smooth motion of easing off the throttle and easing on the brake.**
>
> *Jeff Gordon*

The driver can make this situation worse by mismanaging weight transfer. Turning the steering wheel too harshly or too quickly can make this condition worse, and stabbing or jumping on the brake pedal can have the same negative effect. The driver's use of steering and brakes directly affects how quickly weight transfers forward under braking and laterally during cornering. Smooth, precise use of the controls allows you to manage weight transfer more effectively and avoid some of the handling ills caused by wheel lockup and by applying too much brake while turning the steering wheel.

CORNER ENTRY PATHS DURING BRAKING

Naturally, the shape of the race track dictates the fastest line for entering a corner, but the type of car, its setup, and your situation must also be considered. For example, a car that transfers more weight might need to be driven into a corner in a straighter line to achieve more deceleration. The need to turn must be balanced with the need to brake. The more braking you use, the less traction you have available for steering, so you are limited in how much you can turn the steering wheel. Turn it too much while braking and the car will slide, probably in a push. Your path into a turn can have a major affect on this.

In most cases, the driver's line into a corner begins with heavy braking (primarily in a straight line) followed by a gentle turn-in as brake pedal pressure is slightly reduced. As the car travels deeper into the corner, the steering wheel angle is increased while brake pedal pressure is reduced.

The driver is walking a two-dimensional tightrope in an effort to use 100 percent of the available tire traction. Based on the traction circle theory, some of the traction created by the tires can be used for cornering and some for braking. The trick, and it's truly an art form, is to keep the car on the edge of the circle all the way around the track. How well you do this is a key to speed on the race track. Keeping the car on the edge of adhesion while braking and turning into a corner is the most difficult job of the race driver.

> **Sometimes you'll ride the brake pedal way on into the middle of the corner. Sometimes you're actually almost on the brake and the gas at the same time before you release the gas pedal completely.**
>
> *–Ricky Rudd*

Think of the steering wheel being linked to the brake pedal with a rod. If you brake harder, you must reduce steering wheel lock. Conversely, if you increase steering input, you must reduce pedal pressure on the brakes. In this case, the driver is the rod linking the two systems. Get it right and you're quick. Get it wrong and you're slow.

The path you follow into a turn determines the balance between brake pedal pressure and steering wheel input. If you go in straighter, you can brake harder. If you turn in earlier or increase steering, you will need to brake less. This is one reason to try different lines into a corner. And different cars will need different lines, especially different classes of cars. Additionally, variations in lines will allow you to know what you can and cannot do in a passing situation. How well does an alternate line work? How much traction is available from the racing surface on the alternate line? Know these answers before you try to pass someone off your normal line. Sliding into another car or the wall is not an effective learning method. If crashing is your preferred method of learning, hire a big crew and bring an even bigger checkbook.

LEFT-FOOT BRAKING TECHNIQUE

In the transition from full power to braking, left-foot braking is an important skill to develop. You can make the transition more quickly and more smoothly by left-foot braking. This is the single most important reason to left-foot brake in stock car racing.

The most effective way to left-foot brake is to squeeze on the brake pedal while simultaneously easing off the throttle. Timing is critical. Do not brake hard under full throttle, or excessive heat and brake wear will occur. Make sure you do not ride the brakes when you are not intending to slow. And make sure to lift your right foot completely off the throttle when braking.

It is important to ease off the throttle as you squeeze the brake pedal. Abrupt use of the controls will unsettle the balance of the car, causing handling problems and loss of speed. When the throttle is

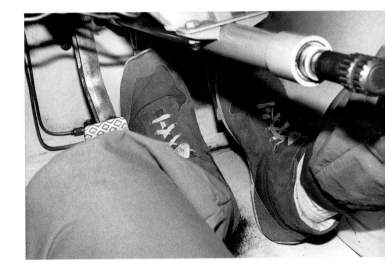

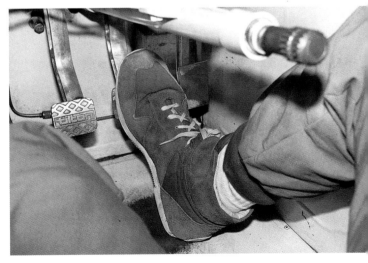

These photos show left-foot versus right-foot braking. You can make smoother transitions from acceleration to braking when left-foot braking. It is good to keep your heel just off the floor when braking to allow smoother motion and better feel.

about halfway released, begin to apply light pressure to the brake pedal. Increase brake pedal pressure quickly as you finish releasing the throttle. The throttle should be fully released before peak braking force is applied. With both pedals, remember to drive as if an egg were between your foot and the pedal. You should be as smooth and fluid as possible.

We have seen the importance of left-foot braking, and here are some tips for its effective use:

1. **Use the ball of your foot on the pedal pad to increase feel for braking forces;**
2. **Keep you heel off the floor to facilitate small changes to brake pedal pressure (modulation);**
3. **Make sure your left foot does not ride the pedal when not intending to slow;**
4. **Begin applying light pressure to the brake pedal as you lift off the gas to take up free play in the pedal system;**
5. **Squeeze the pedal on, don't stab it;**
6. **Ease off the brake pedal in the same way, and do not lift off the pedal abruptly.**

DEVELOPING BRAKING SKILLS

The only true way to understand the relationship between braking, steering, car setup, driving style, and consistency is on the race track. On a test day, a driver should try different amounts of braking and steering lock and work on left-foot braking. The timing between the left foot on the

> **You apply the throttle as you release the brake pedal, going to full throttle in one smooth motion.**
>
> *–Jeff Gordon*

> **When you apply the brake relative to the throttle pedal, release varies from track to track. Depending on how the car transfers weight, when you ease off the gas [throttle], or even what springs you run in the car, the point can vary. There's not a fixed point.**
>
> *–Ricky Rudd*

brake pedal and the right foot on the throttle is the only way to assure solid development of skills.

Begin by braking in a straight line, until lockup occurs. You should be doing this to adjust brake bias anyway. This is the opportunity to develop a feel for the braking limits of the car at maximum braking force in a straight line. Next try different entry lines into each turn on the track, varying the amount of steering and the amount of brake pedal pressure. By trial and error, you will find the best compromise for the track, your driving style, and the car setup. You will also learn alternate lines you can use in racing situations. Be sure to leave plenty of room on the track as a buffer for the inevitable mistakes you will make while learning and tuning the car

As a driver, you need to know four things about your braking system and your braking technique:

1. **The relationship between brake pedal pressure and deceleration;**
2. **The effect of brake pedal modulation (modulation is small pressure adjustments on the brake pedal on deceleration and wheel lockup;**
3. **The relationship between brake pedal pressure and slowing (or stopping) distance;**
4. **The relationship between steering wheel lock angle and brake pedal pressure at the limits of tire traction.**

> **To find the limits of the tire traction under braking, you keep sneaking up on it until you lock the brakes up. First, you have to make sure you have maximum braking power at both ends of the car without it upsetting the car. You try to sneak up on the rear brake bias without it skidding the rear tires.**
>
> *–Ricky Rudd*

Experiment and practice each of these until they are second nature. You will also need to learn to recognize when you make a mistake, so that you can make adjustments quickly, minimize the mistake, and improve your skill. For example, if you apply the brakes too early going into a corner, ease off the pedal some, so that you arrive at the corner at the correct speed. You have already made the braking zone longer than necessary. By braking as hard as normal, you will attain the proper cornering speed too early, or you will slow too much. Each of these scenarios is an additional mistake, making the first mistake worse. By applying less pedal pressure, more speed is carried through the longer braking zone. This eliminates further mistakes and reduces the time lost to a minimum.

EFFECTIVE STEERING TECHNIQUE

Proper use of the steering wheel is a very important driving skill for the stock car racer and is often overlooked and underdeveloped. While many aspects of steering wheel usage have been covered in the braking, we will look at the whole picture here. Keep in mind that turning the front wheels is like applying the brakes. The more steering input applied to the car, the more drag is created, and that slows the car. The goal is always to negotiate a corner at the limit of tire traction on the desired line with the *least* possible amount of steering wheel rotation angle.

The accepted ideal hand position is placement of the left hand at the 9 o'clock position and the right hand at the 3 o'clock position on the steering wheel. This provides the best base for quick movements and the most feedback from forces at the tire

> When you actually turn the steering wheel into a corner, it often depends on the front end settings. Different drivers like different settings. Some drivers just like to relax the grip on the wheel and let the banking turn the car in; others like a street car, where you have to physically turn the steering wheel.
>
> *–Ricky Rudd*

This series of photos shows steering wheel use. In the top photo, note the 3 o'clock and 9 o'clock hand positions. This hand position provides the best control and feedback from the car. The second photo shows the wheel turned nearly 90 degrees. Always use a smooth motion when turning the steering wheel. The last photo shows the wheel turned beyond 90 degrees. The best way to do this is to pass the wheel through one hand with the other hand so that both hands are always on the wheel. With a little practice, this is a very quick and smooth way to turn the wheel when you run out of elbow clearance.

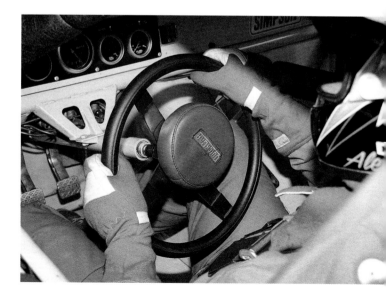

This car is at mid-turn. Note how far the right front wheel is turned. At this point, the driver is no longer adding steering lock and will begin to unwind the steering wheel.

At the exit, the driver begins to accelerate as he unwinds the steering wheel. The more the wheel is unwound, and the straighter the path of the car, the more the car can accelerate.

In these photos, shot on a skid pad, the car is in a steady state of cornering. On a track, this would be mid-turn, where the driver has turned the steering wheel as far necessary, is off the brakes, and has picked up the throttle but is not yet accelerating. In order to accelerate, the driver must unwind the steering to reduce lateral weight transfer, which here is at its maximum. Trying to accelerate with the car at this attitude in a turn would cause a push, or wheelspin. Neither is good for lap times.

contact patch. While many top-level drivers do not use the ideal position, it is best to use the ideal, especially if you are a newcomer.

One of the great controversies concerning race driving techniques is how quickly to rotate the steering wheel. On asphalt ovals, the controversy is unfounded. The wheel should be turned relatively slowly and precisely unless you are taking extreme evasive action or correcting for excessive oversteer. Even then, turning the wheel too quickly reduces the chance of a successful maneuver.

Part of how quickly to turn the wheel relates to tire design and construction. It takes a finite amount of time for cornering forces and tire slip angles to be generated. The steering wheel should never be turned faster than the time needed for tire slip angles to occur. The tire sidewall construction and height are factors determining how fast slip angles build at the tire contact patch. For most stock tires on asphalt, slip angles at the limits of tire traction are fairly high, and the tall sidewalls cause slip angles to build up more slowly than say an Indy or F1 car.

If the steering wheel is moved too abruptly, the tire contact patch will slide before optimum traction is reached. In turn, weight transfers too quickly, causing the tire slip angles to overshoot the optimum angle for maximum cornering force and minimum heat build up. This reduces cornering force and overheats tires because they are forced to operate at a higher than desirable slip angle, adding more heat and reducing cornering speed. If you're braking at the same time you jerk the steering wheel, the loss of traction is abrupt. At the minimum, it will cost time, and it could cause a slide into the wall.

The steering wheel should be rotated in a smooth, precise motion. You will develop a feel for how fast you can rotate the wheel based on the feedback through the steering wheel. You can feel the forces build up. The goal is to turn the wheel as little as possible to drive through a turn at maximum cornering speed on the ideal line. Like any other skill, practice and experience will help you achieve this. When practicing, focus attention on hand movements and feeling what the tire contact patches are doing.

Here the car is near the exit of the turn, with the front wheel turned almost straight ahead. By this point, most cars can be accelerating at full throttle.

A spin this late going into a corner indicates that the driver was using excessive brake pedal pressure while steering. The traction circle dictates the relationship between braking and turning. Here, there was too much brake for the amount of steering or too much steering for the amount of braking.

CORNER ENTRY

As we have seen, coordinating steering wheel rotation with brake pedal pressure is one of the most important skills of the race driver.

> **Every track is different, so you drive into the corner under braking as hard as you can and find a reference point on the wall or track as a marker.**
>
> *–Jeff Gordon*

- Ease off the brake pedal pressure as you begin to turn into a corner;
- Use all of the available tire traction by staying on the circumference of the traction circle;
- Turn the steering wheel slowly into the turn, turning more as you ease off the brakes.

CORNER EXIT

The exit of the corner is the reverse of the entry. As you unwind the steering wheel, you can apply more power. At mid-turn, all the tire traction is used for cornering. As you begin to unwind the steering wheel at the exit, more traction is available to accelerate. How hard you can accelerate is dependent on the track configuration, horsepower, and tire traction. The key is to accelerate as hard as possible without wheel spin. The less you have the steering wheel turned, the more you can accelerate. In the next chapter, we will look at cornering lines to better tie together the elements of cornering, braking, and acceleration.

STEERING-RELATED HANDLING PROBLEMS

Smooth, precise steering wheel movements never cause handling problems. Abrupt, harsh steering inputs by the driver almost always cause

A spin going into a turn can be caused by too much rear brake bias. If this occurs, make sure the brake balance bar (shown) or proportioning valve is properly adjusted.

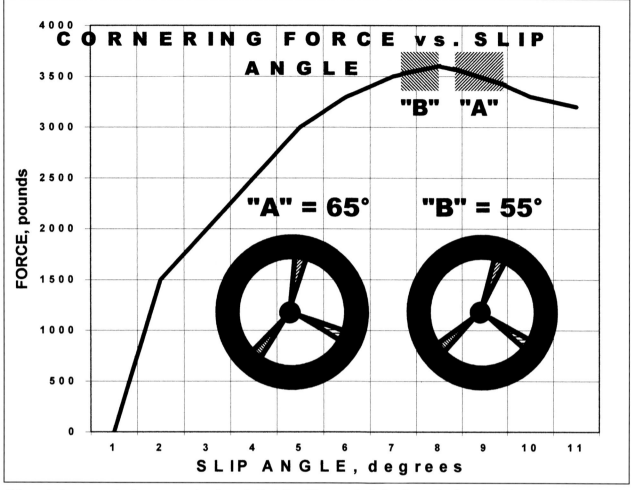

This graph shows cornering force versus tire slip angle. Both A and B are at the limits of cornering force, but driver A has the steering wheel turned farther than driver B. While cornering speed is the same, after several laps, driver A's tires will be more worn and overheated. Thus, his tires will make less traction with time causing a loss of speed. Over a period of many laps, driver B will pull away, just because he drove a smaller slip angle by turning the steering wheel less.

handling problems. Abrupt, jerky steering movements cause weight to transfer abruptly, faster than the shocks can control. Additionally, the tire slip angles cannot keep up, so they overshoot the optimum in an effort to create traction. Both situations can cause reduced traction, especially at the front.

In a steady state in which no braking or acceleration is taking place, the likely outcome is understeer, or push. This further reduces speed. If you are braking or accelerating, the problem is more pronounced and could be either understeer (push) or oversteer (loose). Abrupt steering inputs while braking can cause the unloaded rear tires to lose traction abruptly, or could cause a push by overloading the front tires. Many factors come into play,

but the outcome is the same, lost traction, time, and possibly a slide into the fence.

> To manage tires, try not to spin the rear tires, and try not to turn the steering wheel any more than you have to.
>
> *–Jeff Burton*

A similar scenario plays out if abrupt steering inputs are made while accelerating. Adding steering lock under hard acceleration can cause a push. Although it is less likely, reducing steering lock abruptly under full throttle acceleration can cause oversteer. Additionally, abrupt braking inputs or

Steering Wheel Angle Diagrams

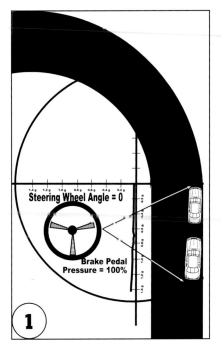

Steering Wheel Angle = 0

Brake Pedal Pressure = 100%

1

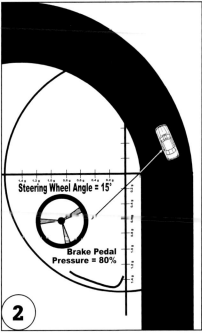

Steering Wheel Angle = 15°

Brake Pedal Pressure = 80%

2

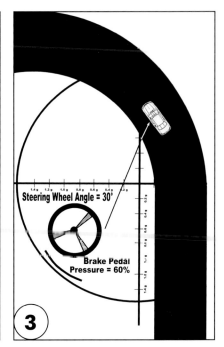

Steering Wheel Angle = 30°

Brake Pedal Pressure = 60%

3

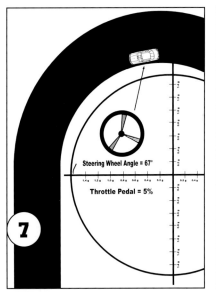

Steering Wheel Angle = 67°

Throttle Pedal = 5%

7

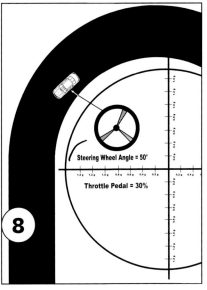

Steering Wheel Angle = 50°

Throttle Pedal = 30%

8

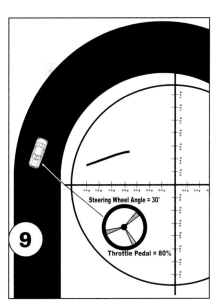

Steering Wheel Angle = 30°

Throttle Pedal = 80%

9

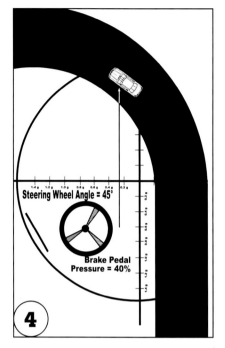

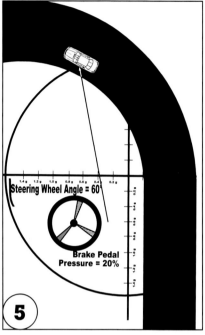

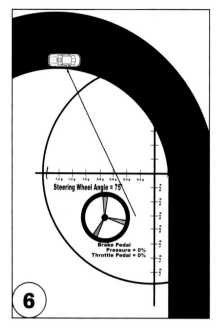

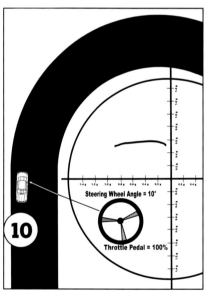

This series of diagrams shows a car at various points around the race track, from the braking zone to the entry of a corner, through the corner, and accelerating out of the corner. Each diagram shows the position of the car on the track, the steering wheel angle, the percentage of throttle or brake pedal application (100 percent is full throttle acceleration or maximum deceleration without wheel lockup) and the related traction circle trace segment. Study the relationship between steering input and use of the brakes and throttle at various points. The angles and percents are not real world, but closely depict the relationship of steering, pedal usage, and track position.

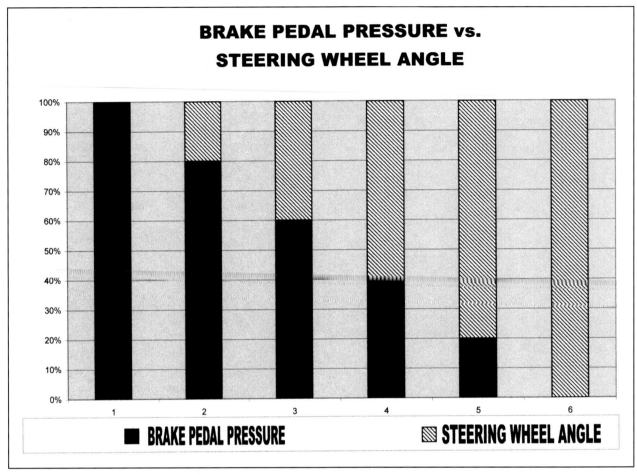

BRAKE PEDAL PRESSURE vs. STEERING WHEEL ANGLE

■ BRAKE PEDAL PRESSURE   ▨ STEERING WHEEL ANGLE

This chart shows the relative balance between brake pedal pressure and steering wheel angle.

throttle applications while steering can cause similar problems. The key here is to have slow hands on the steering wheel and soft feet on the pedals. Smooth and precise are the ideals, not abrupt and jerky. A driver needs to practice smoothness.

THROTTLE PEDAL APPLICATION

The final control is the throttle pedal. Acceleration is the most important element of getting around the track quickly. The throttle pedal is the easiest control to master, but that does not mean that you don't need to pay attention to developing skills for throttle pedal control. Quite the contrary! Abrupt application of the throttle pedal can cost time, wear tires excessively, or even cause a crash.

> **You want to stay on the verge of the tires spinning when accelerating. The way you learn that limit is to press on the gas pedal until the tires spin then back off a little.**
>
> *–Terry Labonte*

> **You can usually go to full throttle about halfway through the exit of the turn, using a pretty quick motion on the throttle, depending on the turn.**
>
> *–Jeff Gordon*

Like the brake pedal, consider the throttle pedal linked to the steering wheel. In this case, you

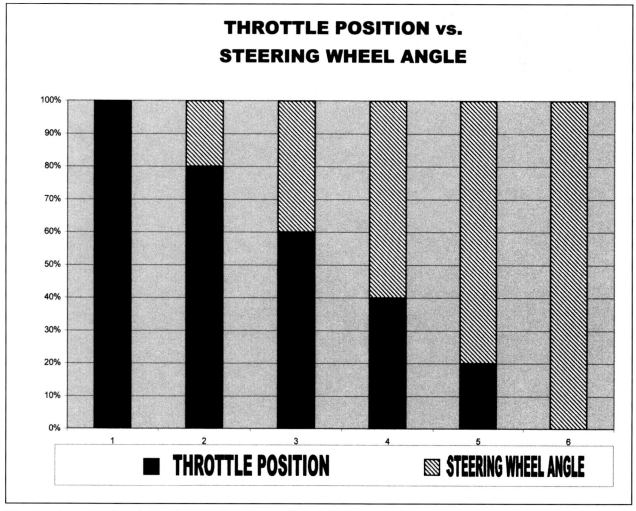

THROTTLE POSITION vs. STEERING WHEEL ANGLE

■ **THROTTLE POSITION**   ▨ **STEERING WHEEL ANGLE**

This chart shows the relative balance between throttle pedal position and steering wheel angle.

can apply more throttle as you reduce steering wheel angle at the exit of a corner. The goal is to accelerate as early as possible, as hard as possible without wheelspin. The corner exit line is a big factor (see the next chapter), but how smoothly you apply the throttle pedal is a more important factor. Ideally, a slight amount (about 10 percent) of wheel spin, is the ideal. More than that, and traction is lost and the tires will overheat, making the problem worse as the laps add up. Practice and experience are paramount for developing these skills.

Keep in mind that track configuration, tire traction, torque of the engine, and corner exit line determine how hard you can accelerate. Changing the line may allow harder acceleration if wheel spin occurs. Finding the best compromise is crucial for all

situations, and changing track conditions may dictate a change in throttle application and line.

A primary goal of the stock car driver should be

> **You can only go as fast as the car will let you go. If you try to go faster than that, that's when you get in trouble.**
>
> *–Jeff Burton*

the smooth, precise, and balanced use of all the controls. These skills often prove to be the difference between a fast qualifying time and not making the show, or a top 10 finish instead of being lapped. Success comes with developing these skills.

Cornering Lines, Braking Points, and Acceleration

T he path around the race track— where to brake, turn, and accelerate—are all critical for fast laps. To best understand the priorities, and how to determine the optimum line around a track, we will use numerous illustrations and captions in this chapter.

LINES AND THE TRACTION CIRCLE

The driver's ability to use maximum tire traction in every section of the track is paramount to success. Keeping the tires on the edge of the traction circle is the goal, and driving the optimum line around the race track is one determining factor. Balancing steering inputs combined with brake and throttle pedal use, along with the right line around the track is crucial.

The actual line around a track, especially entering a turn, is *less* important than the need to stay at the edge of the traction circle. Many alternate entry lines that allow use of maximum traction can be used. The options are more limited on the exit.

Jeff Gordon is one of the best drivers at selecting the fastest lines on the track. The fast line almost always changes during the course of the race. Finding that line or sometimes developing that line is essential for success. Here, he runs the fast line exiting a turn at one of the most famous NASCAR short tracks, Bristol Motor Speedway. *Nigel Kinrade*

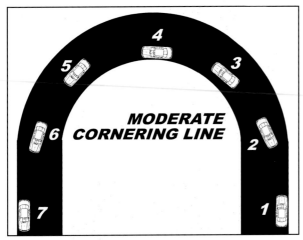

This is the moderate cornering line, the one that works on most tracks. Turn-in is not too early or too late, and the exit line allows for early acceleration.

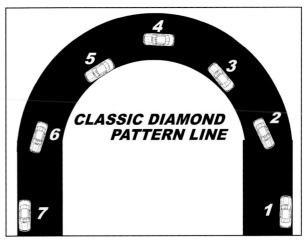

The classic diamond pattern is shown here. This line through a turn allows a straighter line into and out of the corner, but requires more slowing in mid-turn, where the car is rotated for the exit. This line works well on a very flat, tight track, especially with high-horsepower cars.

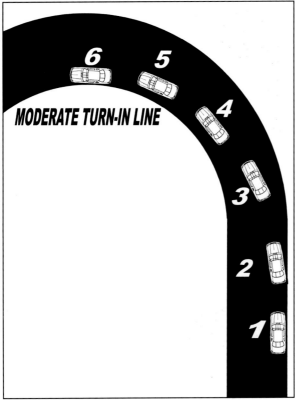

The moderate turn-in line is the most common. At 1, the driver is braking at the limit of traction. At 2, the brake pedal pressure is eased, and the driver begins to turn in to the corner. No. 3 sees more steering and less brake as the driver moves to the middle of the track on the way to the inside. At 4, additional steering and very moderate braking take place and by No. 5, the driver is off the brakes and using maximum steering lock. The throttle pedal is picked up at 6, but no acceleration takes place, as the driver balances weight on the chassis in preparation to accelerate out of the corner.

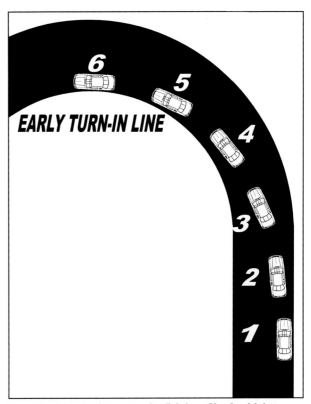

Here, the driver begins to turn in slightly at No. 1, with less than maximum braking. At 2, 3, and 4, the car is lower on the track, which makes this a good line for defending position, as well as to attempt a braking pass underneath another car. Because the entry line is straighter, the driver must rotate the car more between 4 and 5, with the brake pedal released. At 6, the throttle is picked up, as in the moderate entry line.

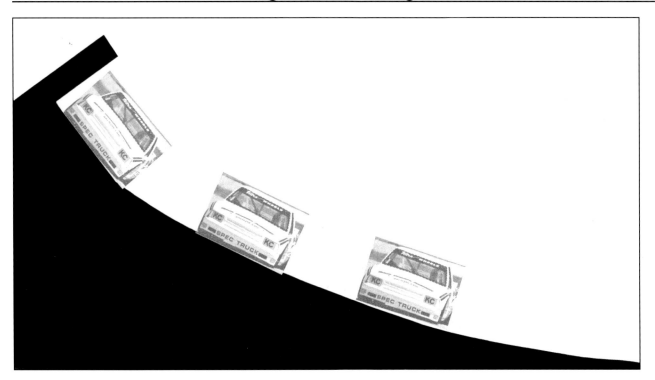

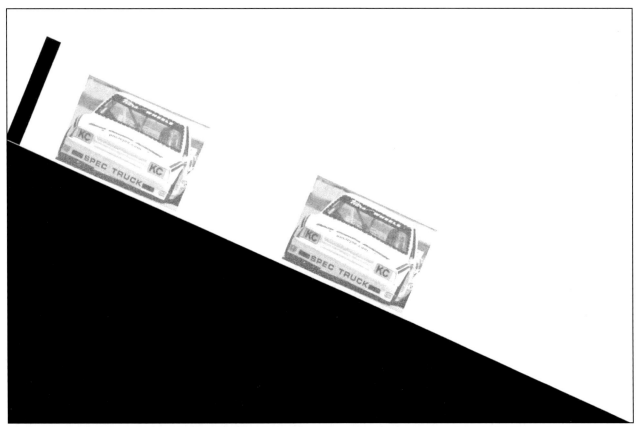

The banking shown above is the same across the width of the race track, so there is no advantage from the banking angle inside or outside. The illustration on the top shows multiple banking angles. The steepest banking will be the fastest, unless the width of the track makes the high groove line too long for a lap time advantage. Often tracks with multiple banking angles allow side-by-side racing for many laps, because the higher but longer outside groove doesn't offer an advantage over the lower but shorter inside groove.

LINES AND BANKING ANGLES

The fastest line around a track varies, based on its geometric configuration as well as the banking. Banking angles vary, or where the low part of the track is flat, the fastest line is usually the line that allows the use of the steepest banking angle through the turns. In some cases, where the track uses multiple banking angles, more than one line may be optimum, especially in a racing situation. Segment times and experience are the only true way to determine the fast line relative to banking angle.

Apexes are more critical on a road course than an oval. In general, the apex is the point where you are closest to the inside of the turn. On a high banked track, there may be no apex. On a tight flat track, you may need to apex twice (a classic diamond pattern), once going into the turn, once exiting.

BRAKING POINTS

One of the most important spots on the track is the place you apply the brakes. At that spot, you determine the speed you plan to take the corner and how much distance it will take to reduce speed

> **You use hard brake pedal pressure on the straightaway, and as you get into the corner you use lighter pedal pressure.**
>
> *–Ricky Rudd*

> **As you get to the braking zone on a short track, you start to look for an imaginary apex where you want to clip with your left front tire.**
>
> *–Ricky Rudd*

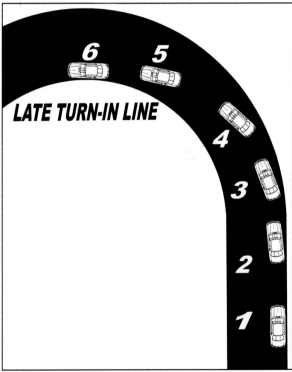

The late turn-in line is more like a classic road racing line. The single advantage is that braking can occur later, but the turn-in is more abrupt. This line leaves the driver very vulnerable to attack in a racing situation. This line is best used for a turn where the exit is less than 90 degrees as on a trioval.

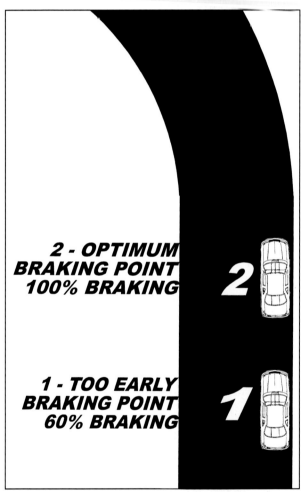

If a driver begins to brake too early, as in No. 1 in the illustration, minimal time will be lost if the driver uses less braking. The goal is to reach the turn-in point, where the driver rotates the car, at the same speed as if braking occurred at the optimum point (No. 2).

This vehicle entered the turn too hot and slid up the track. A little too much rear brake bias or too much steering lock caused a sideways slide. Any more speed and the truck would have spun. The edge between the perfect entry and overdriving is very narrow. The excess speed coming in here was only 2 or 3 miles per hour.

The minimal amount of steering lock on the front wheels indicates a fairly straight line into the corner under braking. This allows considerable braking force to be used. As the driver gets deeper into the corner, brake pedal pressure will be reduced and steering lock increased. The traction circle will dictate the ratio between steering and braking, and it's the driver's job to stay as close to the edge of that circle as possible.

This driver is just beginning to turn into the corner under braking. Here, the driver eases off the brake pedal slightly as the steering wheel lock is increased.

> **Reference points on the race track are extremely important. Every race track has different reference points that you have in your memory, so that every time you go to a track you're basing every lap on those points.**
>
> *–Jeff Gordon*

from maximum to the desired cornering speed. Brake too early and you slow down too much. Brake too late and you carry too much speed into the corner. You will be forced to alter your line, scrub off speed, or even get into the wall. Acute judgment and execution is needed to accomplish these tasks at the limit of traction.

TRACK OUT POINTS

Once the car passes the apex and begins to exit the corner, the driver begins to unwind the steering wheel at the track out point. It is here that you ease on the throttle, driving a line out to the wall that allows maximum acceleration out of the turn and down the straight. The goal is to find a line that will allow full throttle application at the earliest moment. You must find a balance between cornering and acceleration. Unwinding the steering as you accelerate

This line is not the fastest around the track. However, in traffic situations in which cornering speed is slower than usual, it can prove useful. This line allows the driver to brake late and accelerate early. The driver can actually begin to accelerate between 5 and 6, so getting a run on slower cars down the next straight is much easier. Using this line when a car is close behind is an open door for a pass.

These photos show the truck almost to mid-turn. This is the point where the driver is just releasing the brake pedal and making the last few degrees of steering input. The attitude and positioning of this vehicle is nearly perfect.

harder is necessary, but you also need to stay on the track and avoid the wall at the exit. The optimum line out of the turn will allow you to do this.

OPTIMUM LINES FOR ENTERING A TURN

The optimum line entering a turn depends on several factors, but in all cases the most important is

> During the race, I like to hear my lap time every lap over the radio. I use that lap time to fine-tune adjustments to the way I drive the corner. I may drive in deeper and use more brake, or may let off earlier and not use any brake or change the line by 3 or 4 feet toward the top or the bottom of the track. You're always searching during the race. The lap times help.
>
> *–Ricky Rudd*

staying on the edge of the traction circle at the limits of adhesion. These factors affect the optimum line:

- **Type of car**
- **Setup of car**
- **Type of track configuration**
- **Track condition**
- **Banking angle**
- **Location of best available traction (high or low groove)**
- **Driver preference**
- **Racing situation (passing or defending)**

You can drive several different lines with more braking force and less steering at the entry, or more steering and less braking.

OPIMUM LINES FOR EXITING A TURN

The same criteria used for entering a turn apply to the exit line, but the options are fewer because full-throttle acceleration as early as possible is impor-

continued on page 48

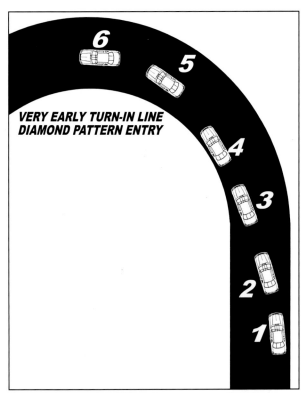

The very early turn-in or diamond pattern entry allows late braking and a straighter run into the corner. The driver actually begins to rotate the car at **No. 1** before braking in many cases. Braking begins as the car approaches **No. 2**, but since the path is almost straight, braking is very close to the maximum. At **5**, the driver must rotate the car more abruptly to be able to pick up the throttle by **No. 6**.

The very early turn-in defensive line is like the diamond pattern from **No. 1** to **No. 4**. The driver must slow more by **No. 4** and begin to rotate the car there. The steering input is less abrupt, and the car is right down to the inside of the track, in order to defend position. An attack would have to come from the outside, which is much less likely to work than a pass to the inside.

This entry line under braking is the moderate line, providing a good balance between braking force and steering inputs.

This truck is a little high going into the corner. This is a good line if a push is present, if the track is slippery down low, or if the banking angle is more advantageous.

This tight exit line allows the car to get the straightest run off the corner under hard acceleration. Note the tire marks showing the ideal exit path in this case.

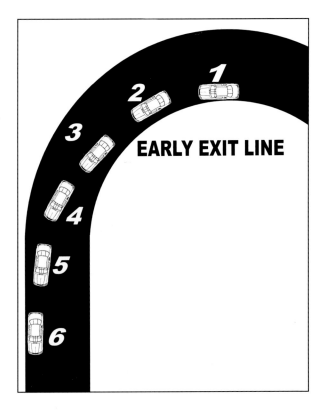

EARLY EXIT LINE

To find the fast line for a given setup, you try different things. Whatever's fastest is what you do.

–Jeff Burton

If you're a tenth of a second off the pace, start experimenting. Try different things, see if there is a way to make your car go faster.

–Jeff Burton

The early exit line works best on tracks with wide radius turns and high banks, or both. This is a fast exit line as long as wheelspin is not a problem during hard acceleration out of the corner. At 1, the driver picks up the throttle without acceleration. Steering lock is reduced at No. 2 and acceleration begins. From No. 3 to No. 5, more throttle is applied, and steering lock is reduced. By No. 5, full throttle acceleration should be taking place. At 6, the car is straight and running close to the wall at full throttle.

This car is taking a low exit line out of a corner. The front wheels are almost straight so hard acceleration is taking place. Since this four-cylinder car is low powered, a higher, earlier exit line would work even better, because wheelspin is not an issue.

Here, the car is exiting a corner under acceleration. Note that the driver is using some steering lock, so the car is still turning. A smooth throttle application will allow this. At the next point on the corner exit, the car is at full throttle exiting Turn Two on to back straight curve. When there is no straight between corners, it is important to drive on an arc that allows maximum acceleration. Also note that the banking angle low on the track is much flatter than in the middle of the track.

The lateral position of this truck is nearly perfect for the type of track. If the truck were any lower, the inside wheels would be positioned near the berm, where the banking angle of the track is almost flat.

This truck is just past midpoint in the turn. The driver is unwinding the wheel and beginning to accelerate. At this point, the path of the truck should be arcing toward the outside wall.

continued from page 44

tant. The goal is to use as much throttle as possible without wheel spin. The straighter the car is pointed, the easier this can be accomplished. Higher horsepower cars will take a different exit line than lower horsepower cars where wheelspin is less likely.

FINDING THE FASTEST LINE

The fastest line produces the fastest qualifying lap. In a racing situation, the fastest line allows you to pass or defend position. Finding the fastest line for various circumstances takes work. Use lap times and detailed records while trying different lines. Take segment time (see the chapter on finding speed), talk to other drivers and watch them, or follow them if possible.

ALTERNATE LINES
FOR CHANGING TRACK CONDITIONS

When track conditions change, you must change your lines as well. A heavily used groove or line typ-

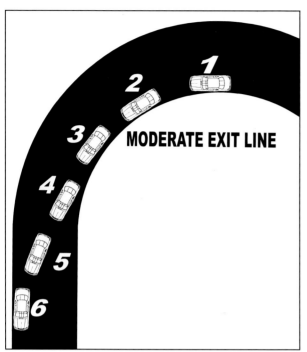

The moderate exit line gives a straighter shot out of the corner, allowing greater acceleration. At each point from No. 2 to 5, acceleration is harder and steering wheel lock is less than in the moderate exit line. This line works well on tighter or less steeply banked tracks or with less horsepower.

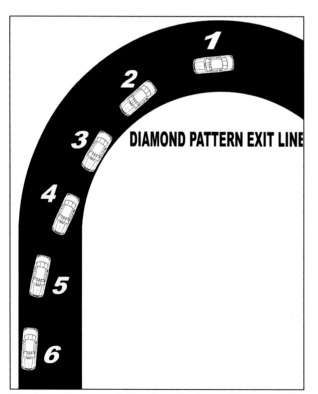

The diamond pattern exit line allows for the straightest run off the corner, so that more acceleration is possible. This is often the fastest line on a track with very tight, flat turns.

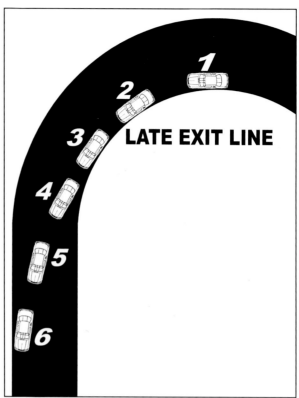

At each point from No. 3 to 5, the car is straighter than in the earlier exit line examples. This allows more acceleration, due to less steering input. This line works best on a very tight, flat track, or anywhere wheel spin occurs with hard acceleration. This is also a good defensive line to keep following cars from getting a run on the straight. In addition, it's an effective way to pass when the car in front slides up the race track in mid-turn.

Racing is about running the car right to the edge. The way you find the edge of tire traction in the turns is to sneak up on the edge. It's a little harder today in Winston Cup racing, because we're limited to three tires on the first day. Your first laps on the track are one of your three sets of tires. You don't have time to go out and play around to get your speed up; you have to go pretty hard. Generally, you set the car up with a little bit of push to begin with then back the push out.

–Ricky Rudd

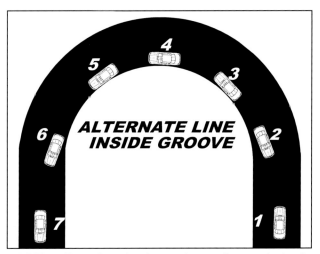

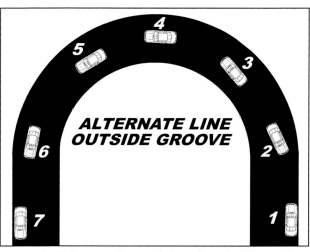

A & B These illustrations show how to alternate lines running in a low groove and a high groove. These variations of standard lines work on a banked track in which the banking angle varies, or when track conditions change and more traction is available in one groove. A high or low groove line is often used on a superspeedway.

The modified is at the midpoint of the turn. The driver has turned the steering to its maximum angle and balanced the car with the throttle, but is accelerating. Note the maximum body roll and the level chassis fore and aft.

ically provides decreasing amounts of traction as the race progresses. When the groove slows down, you must go outside the groove to find a new faster line. Watch what other drivers do, but most important, practice a variety of lines, check segment and lap times and see where you gain or lose time. Study the track surface and note changes when cars begin to move the groove up or down the track.

ALTERNATE LINES
FOR PASSING AND DEFENDING

When the racing situation changes (passing/defending), you need to be able to alter your line to make a pass or fend off a challenger. When you are learning, watch other drivers in racing situations to see how they handle other cars and situations, and practice using alternate lines as discussed above.

Study the illustrations in this chapter to get a feel for the fast lines, alternate lines, what happens going into a turn, in mid-turn, and exiting a turn. Always remember how important using maximum traction is at all times. And keep in mind how you need to use the controls effectively to accomplish all of this. Finally, practice, practice, practice! Seat time with a solid practice plan is the only way you will truly understand the limit, because that takes feel, something we cannot diagram here. Besides, driving practice ain't like spelling practice!

> **As the tires wear and get hotter, that has a tendency to change the line.**
>
> *–Terry Labonte*

> **Some tracks, the line stays the same as the race progresses. Other tracks, the line will change. It really depends on the asphalt, the tires, and track configuration. No two tracks are the same.**
>
> *–Terry Labonte*

This exit line allows maximum acceleration with a minimum of steering wheel angle.

The front straightaway at this track is very short. The driver is still arcing toward the outside wall as he approaches the start/finish line. This line will allow the best acceleration out of the last corner, but means that the car never stops turning left, at least a little.

This driver has just increased throttle pedal pressure to full throttle exiting a turn. Note the chassis squat under maximum acceleration.

This mid-turn shot shows a perfectly balanced car at maximum steering wheel angle and a balanced throttle with no acceleration.

This car has the perfect line exiting the corner. Note that the front wheels are nearly straight, ready for full-throttle acceleration.

Using all of the track is important. On the straights, running close to the wall allows maximum acceleration exiting turns.

Building and Maintaining Concentration

Realizing maximum concentration potential and maintaining a high level of concentration over the entire length of a race is paramount for success. Even if a driver has excellent racing aptitude and superior car control skills, a driver won't be able put in his or her best performance if he or she can't concentrate. The top professional drivers have the ability to simultaneously manage many tasks—steering, line selection, available traction, car position, traffic position, radio communications, and other factors—because of their concentration ability. In addition, the greater a driver's concentration, the greater the ability to rise to challenges at the end of the race.

Twelve laps into the feature, you are leading. You know that the car behind you is very fast, so you check the mirrors to see his position. As you come off Turn Two, you wonder where and when he will attack. You're just not sure that you can fend off the assault. As you approach Turn Three, you get into the corner too hot, slide up higher than you had planned in mid-turn, and the car behind you gets underneath you at the exit of Turn Four. Your little inner voice clicks on, telling you exactly how you screwed up the corner and what a fool you are for letting the other car get by so easily. While you listen to the little voice, two more

In order to have a shot at victory, a competitive driver must be able to concentrate over the entire race distance. Furthermore, car-control skills and racecraft are worth little if a driver can't maintain a high level of concentration. Dale Earnhardt had a mental capacity that allowed him to concentrate on several aspects of car-control, tactics, and strategy at once. His ability to concentrate at the limit made him one of the greatest drivers of all time. *Nigel Kinrade*

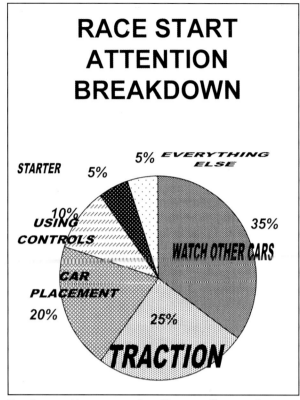

RACE START ATTENTION BREAKDOWN

Here is a graphic representation of how to utilize attention at the start of a race. This will change throughout the race along with the drivers priorities.

A driver needs to have a concentration plan before strapping on the helmet and heading out to the track. Setting a priority list for race driving is essential for getting the most out of the driver. NASCAR's top drivers, like Jeff Burton, have a priority list and a concentration plan that have been finely honed over years of competition. *Nigel Kinrade*

cars go by, one under braking into Turn One, the other follows it through in mid-corner. You begin to feel like an incompetent race driver.

This scenario is all too common in life, let alone racing. The problem is not competency, but one of focusing attention. Concentration is a major factor for success on the race track. But how you concentrate, and on what, is just as important.

CONCENTRATION

To concentrate is to direct one's thoughts or attention to a particular task. Pure concentration should bypass the verbalized thought process, which is too cumbersome and slow. The race driver must process too much data too quickly to allow time for verbalized thought processes to take place. The little voice must be quieted for the efficient flow of data from the senses through the brain and back to the muscles that respond. In essence, concentration is nothing more than paying acute attention to what you re doing *right now!*

In auto racing, the need to pay attention is of the highest priority. At any given instant, a driver must monitor feedback from the car through the steering, brakes, throttle, and the seat of the pants. In addition, the driver must take in visual data and analyze it; monitor the positions of other cars and possible passing or defensive situations that may be developing; and monitor other car systems and information from the crew and track workers. The driver must also be aware of potential hazards. All of this must be accomplished with extreme forces acting on the body, in conditions that are very disruptive to concentration (heat, noise, vibration), while undergoing the physical exertion of a marathon runner. Simply stated, the need to pay attention in a race car is vital, and the environment is extremely hostile.

DEVELOPING CONCENTRATION SKILLS

A driver's ability to concentrate on the job is critical for success and safety. Breaches in concentration make the driver slow and inconsistent. A driver who fails to concentrate for the duration of an event will lose pace or fade, or worse yet, get into the fence.

ATTENTION SKILLS

Like most skills, concentration can be developed and enhanced with practice. Some individuals are blessed with a high natural ability to remain focused for long periods of time. Others must work at it. If you have the attention span of a grasshopper, you should probably work on improving your attention span. There are several ways to do this.

Any game or activity that requires continuous concentration will help you to improve these skills. Using visual imagery or mental rehearsal is great for concentration practice. Try running an entire race mentally to see how well you maintain concentration. Games like chess and activities like reading or meditation are also very helpful. Among the best resources are video games and computer simulations. While most games are helpful, the new generation of auto racing games is the most fun for the racer. Most importantly, they can be used to improve concentration skills. While they may not develop your physical skills for driving, they will help you to become more skilled.

When you work on concentration skills, try the following tips. Practice sessions should last as long as a race. If you have trouble concentrating, start out with short sessions, and increase the length as skills improve. Practice often, three to four times a week, especially in the off-season. Note any outside distractions that break your concentration; see if patterns emerge. If your concentration is broken, try to get back into the flow quickly. If you use mental rehearsal or video games, you may want to wear your driving gear while practicing. While developing your ability to pay attention is crucial, it is only half the battle. Knowing when and where to focus your attention is equally important.

FOCUSING ATTENTION

At any given moment, a driver has several focus-of-attention options, as well as the distraction of extraneous inputs. In a race, the driver must analyze visual data, sense and analyze forces, determine the line through corners, watch traffic, watch for flags or lights, listen to the crew on the radio, monitor temps and pressures, make tactical decisions, and manage tires. There's a lot to think about. It is very important to know when and what to focus your attention on. To manage your ability to stay focused on the most important elements requires a plan and establishing priorities. You can't do this on the track because you just do not have enough time to think about it. You must know them thoroughly, so your priorities are always second nature.

ATTENTION PRIORITY MENU

A driver must focus attention on several different things at once, but some are clearly more important than others. Here is a list of areas requiring attention from the driver at any given time.

- **Traction**
- **Position of vehicle on the race track**
- **Control usage (steering, brakes, throttle)**
- **Location of competitor's cars**
- **Race tactics**
- **Race strategy**
- **Starter, corner workers, and lights**
- **Crew on radio or pit board**
- **Gauges**
- **Environment surrounding the race track**
- **Breathing and other physical factors affecting the driver**

At any moment, attention must be focused on all of these factors. What changes is the actual amount of attention spent on each one at a given

During practice or testing, attention priorities are very different than during qualifying or a race. Understanding different ways to divide attention at different times and for different aspects of racing is a key factor in developing race-winning concentration skills.

time. If all of your attention is spent on any single factor, trouble is likely to occur.

EXCEEDING CONCENTRATION CAPACITY— THE RED MIST

When a driver focuses his or her attention, or too much of it, on a single factor to the exclusion of all others, a phenomenon often referred to as the "red mist" occurs. A mist clouds the driver's judgment because only certain factors are observed. This often occurs in the heat of battle, when a driver focuses totally on the other car being engaged in a close race. This tunnel vision approach is rarely effective and very dangerous on the race track. The driver must learn to spend the attention for all of the factors determined to be priorities; then the driver must decide which factor is most important at any given time, paying the greatest attention to that factor. Here's an example.

START OF THE RACE

All of the factors listed previously are important at the start, but knowing the location of the cars around you is the most important, closely followed by traction and the placement of your car on the track.

Let's say that you have 100 percent attention to devote to racing the car. At the start, you may use 35 percent of your attention on watching other cars, 25 percent on traction, 20 percent on where you place your car, 10 percent on using the controls, 5 percent on the starter (or crew on the radio), and 5 percent on a slight awareness of everything else. While a general awareness must be maintained on all factors, some are very low priorities as the race starts. As the race progresses, your priorities will shift. In fact, they will shift at different points on the race track.

SHIFTING PRIORITIES

As you approach a turn without traffic, your priorities shift. Now you must pay greater attention to traction, brake, steering usage, and the path you want to drive around the turn. Once you begin slowing, your priorities shift to picking up the throttle and unwinding the steering wheel. And traction remains a high priority. Even then some awareness of the corner workers, other cars, and general environment is important.

If you are in the same situation and in traffic as well, watching other cars may take the top spot on your priority list. And when you are challenging for the lead, planning a pass may be your highest concentration priority. Understanding the most important

Bobby Labonte, like many other drivers, heightens his concentration as the race nears. Many drivers play a mental film of the race in their heads before the start of the race. This technique allows drivers to anticipate and deal with many possible contingencies. *Nigel Kinrade*

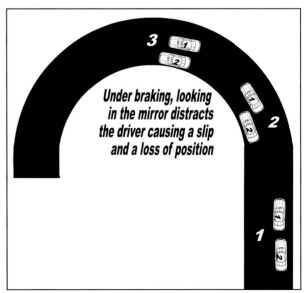

Under braking, looking in the mirror distracts the driver causing a slip and a loss of position

Learning to shift priorities is crucial and doing it at the wrong time is costly. As illustrated above, the driver looks in the mirror at the wrong time and the distraction causes a loss of position.

> **Working lapped traffic that's not so cooperative can interfere with concentration. When a guy is several laps down and you're running with the leaders, and he lets the leader by easily but wants to race with you, that's distracting.**
>
> *–Ricky Rudd*

priorities at a given time is very important; being able to have a fluid plan that allows priorities to shift as needed is equally important. Going into a race meeting without a plan to effectively focus your attention leads to problems on the race track. You must have a concentration plan for practice, qualifying, and the race. Racing without a plan is like having no setup or maintenance plan for the race car. If you have no plan, it is easy to fall victim to someone else's plan, and rarely does a competitor's plan call for you to win the race.

CREATING A PLAN

The first step to effective use of attention on the race track is to create a plan. The plan should include a list of the factors you feel are important priorities, and how these priorities will shift during an event. What items require the most attention before you get into the car? What requires attention during hot laps? Will qualifying see the priorities shift again? During a race, how will priorities change? And where do you focus your attention at different points on the race track? By creating a plan with these elements, you will develop a real sense for your personal priorities, where to spend your attention most effectively, and how to shift attention as needed.

Once you have the plan, implement it by practicing. Use racing video games or visualize different scenarios on the track and practice focusing attention where you feel it needs to be spent. If you do this, when you hit the race track, focusing and shifting attention to your most important priorities will be second nature.

Jeff Gordon holds off Jimmy Hensley and Davey Allison in the 1993 Hanes 500. Gordon is able to hold the lead because he is monitoring and managing a number of different tasks at once˜braking points, steering points, available traction, line selection, and the traffic behind. *Nigel Kinrade*

Finding More Speed

Y ou're a half-second off the pace and desperate to find the time. The harder you try and the more you think about finding speed, the more time you lose. The key to finding that speed is to forget about finding the speed. Focus attention on using the controls as smoothly and perfectly as possible. And slow down so that you drive every inch of the race track as perfectly as possible, on the right line, braking at the exact point necessary and picking up the throttle at the right place. Then you will automatically start to go faster. It's really that simple. But there is one important tool you can use to help the process. Work on different parts of the track and take segment times.

SEGMENT TIMING

Lap after lap, your primary competitor is 1/10 second faster than you. You can always catch him under braking going into the turns, stay with him through mid-turn, but lose ground at the exit. You're sure he has a horsepower advantage, but your crew chief thinks otherwise. The crew chief decides to take segment times. He divides Turn One and Two into segments; the first covers from the braking point to the middle of the turns while the second covers from the middle of the turns to the point where the cars are no longer turning. The crew chief times each car for 20 laps in each segment. He then averages the segment times. He finds that you are consistently 0.05 second

In order to find more speed, many drivers break down their laps into component parts or segments. The segment times are taken so that the driver can determine where time is being gained or lost. A driver should analyze how he or she is operating the controls and how the car is behaving in the various segments of the track. This exercise will allow the driver to formulate a plan for faster driving and resolve driving problems. *Nigel Kinrade*

faster in the entry segment, but you are 0.10 second slower on the exit segment. He notices that the other driver is off the brakes and on the power earlier than you. A change in technique could mean faster laps on the race track. Segment times are a tool to help you determine the effect of changes to the car or your technique.

PRIORITIES FOR SEGMENT TIMING

Races are won by getting to the checkered flag before the competition, not by setting fastest laps. Different mindsets are required for winning races and setting fast laps for qualifying. Both are important, but must be differentiated. By the same token, the fastest car on one segment of the track does not win the pole. The first priority should be fast laps. But to achieve fast laps, segment times can be very useful.

First of all: What is a lap time? It is data that offer us some useful information. If you went faster on a given lap, the lap time is the information that tells you how much. The fact that you went faster could mean that you tried a different line, drove harder, had less traffic, made a productive change to the car prior to the session, or encountered improved track conditions. The change or changes you made to go faster cannot be determined from the lap time alone. The data are insufficient. Additional input must come from other sources: the driver, crew, and so on.

How many times has this happened to you? You enter the pits after a session, and your crew tells you that your time was a half-second faster on lap 5. It's your best time ever, and you are justifiably pleased. But what occurred on lap 5 that caused you to go faster? If you identified the changes in your technique, you can make real progress. If you have not, the next fast lap you achieve will be as random as the first one.

The second priority is to have a plan, so that the results are quantifiable. This is even more important when taking segment times. If you change tire pressure, you make a note of the change *and* the effect (hopefully). The same applies to the driver making changes in technique—lines, steering points, braking points, etc. The simple fact that you went faster is not very useful unless you can repeat the fast lap. Knowing the change that allowed the fast lap will allow more fast laps, and possibly even faster laps.

The third priority is the time through a segment of the track, relative to overall lap times in the context of qualifying, and relative to the segment location and strategy for a race. A faster segment time is only beneficial if it improves the overall lap time. In a race, however, being faster in a given segment may be more important than lap times, if it allows a given race strategy to be implemented successfully.

SEGMENT TIMING GAME PLAN

It is important to establish a plan for recording segment times before a session begins. Only one evaluation per session should be tried. It is important to determine what effect a certain change made on segment times and on overall lap times. Setup changes to the car or driving technique changes should be undertaken individually in a given session, but not both. If the driver wants to try a new line or other change in technique, it should be limited to one turn, so that the overall effect of the change can be determined. The purpose is to eliminate any variables in the situation.

It should be noted that segment times are less useful if a driver is learning a new track or a new car. Segment times are most valuable when the driver is familiar with the car and the track and is able to run consistent laps close to the limit. This applies equally to car modifications or changes to driving techniques.

The types of changes to driver techniques that can be evaluated with segment times that include lines, braking points, and alternate lines for passing. The fast line (the geometrically largest radius) through a turn requires the least steering lock, and hence the least tire scrub, but the car travels farther. Which is faster? Or is a compromise best? Segment times will quickly sort out the best approach.

SELECTING SEGMENTS

Two criteria are used when selecting segments. First, a track segment should be selected where the car is experiencing a specific problem, or where the driver could gain time. Second, segments should incorporate significant portions of the race track. The entire track should be broken into segments, but care should be used in the selection process. The number of segments should correlate to the track configuration, the goals of the test day or session, the time available, and the equipment and personnel available. Attempting to evaluate segment times from 10 areas of the track without the time or people to collect and analyze the data leads to information overload. A small amount of useful data is much more beneficial than reams of paper that no one has time to review.

When selecting segments and establishing the pretest plan, it is best to prioritize each segment relative to its value and the purpose of the session. For example, the most important segment may be leading onto a straight. Or, a driver may have a problem in a given turn; that may be the most important segment. On cars with adjustable aerodynamics, more downforce may be the fastest way around the track, but may cause enough drag so that passing is difficult on long straights. Segment times on fast sections can help determine what works best.

Segments can be straightaways, entire turns, portions of turns, or even half of the track. The key is to use segments as a tool to go faster. The segments are created as part of a plan; the plan is not created because you happen to have segment times.

TAKING SEGMENT TIMES

Taking segment times requires a timing device, track reference points, visibility of both ends of the segment, and a method to keep notes. More sophisticated methods, data acquisition systems, video cameras, or a computer, are available. The use of radios can make segment timing more useful, allowing a driver to try more than one segment per lap, because the crew can remind the driver of the changes to make before arriving at the segment.

Accuracy of times is crucial. An error of even 0.05 second can negate the usefulness of the times. Keep in mind that if the track is broken into only four segments, an error of 0.05 second on a segment is like 0.2 second mistake on the full track. In any segment, 0.05 second is a very important amount of time to gain or lose, especially for a skilled driver in a well-prepared car.

In addition to noting segment times, an observer should also take notes on lines, braking points, apexes, mistakes, the set of the chassis, and even the squeal of the tires on each lap. This can be correlated with the data provided by the driver. If a radio is used, someone should take notes covering

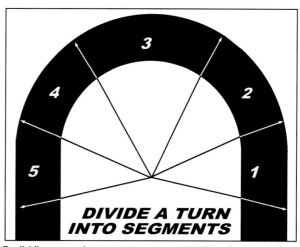

DIVIDE A TURN INTO SEGMENTS

By dividing a turn into segments, you can analyze changes, both to car and driving style, to determine what works best. Here are sample segments, but customize your segment timing to suit your needs.

what the driver did on a given lap and the driver's remarks about what occurred. This information can be extremely valuable.

EVALUATING SEGMENT TIMES

Naturally, evaluation of the data is the most important part of segment timing. On the surface it appears that the only evaluation needed is what was fastest segment and how it occurred. While in many cases this is true, there are occasions when a faster segment may be detrimental to fast lap times, or to the tactics of winning the race.

Often, a segment speed is not important to overall lap times, but the following segment is crucial. We may need to sacrifice speed in the first segment, so that the car is set up to gain exit speed into a straight. This is the scenario in the opening example.

First, we create a corner segment. We will time a car from turn-in point to exit on a variety of lines, and we will soon learn that the geometrically perfect line, allowing the largest radius through the turn, is the fastest. If we discount the following straightaway and subsequently the entire lap, overall performance is affected negatively, even though speed is found on a segment of the race track. If we were to create a smaller segment (turn-in point to the apex) within this turn, we would again find a great increase in speed if we take an early turn-in and early apex approach. But driving off the track at the exit is not the way to make the

Rusty Wallace and all of the top professional drivers have developed a fine sense for speed at each point of a particular race track. Here, Wallace rails through a corner at the First Union 400 at North Wilkesboro in 1996. *Nigel Kinrade*

fastest lap times. Each segment must be taken in the context of all other segments.

Another area where segment times can be misused is the preparation of race strategy. The goal of the race, which is to win or place as high as possible, often requires different car settings and a different driving style or at least different priorities. In close races, a driver is often pressured by competitors for the duration, and the last lap often decides the outcome. It is important to make a plan for that last lap, especially the last turn before the checkered flag. An advantage here can win the race, even if speed is sacrificed in other segments of the track.

One of the most important uses of segment times is rarely used by most competitors. Segment times for alternate lines will help to win races. By finding the fastest way around, then trying alternate lines where passing or defending are likely to occur, a driver and crew can evaluate what line, or lines, will result in the least amount of lost time. On a tight quarter-mile track, getting the car to work on the outside often gains benefits in traffic.

Segment times are a great tool, but no one has won a pole with the fastest time in the seventh segment. Use segment times to try new techniques, learn new lines, and test new car setups. Establish a plan and stick to it, so that the most is gained from the effort, either an improvement or a setback. Either will provide valuable information. Collecting too much data can cause confusion and create more problems than it can solve. Work within the available time frame and logistics. Analyze the data carefully, and make decisions based on the goal, either qualifying or the race. The final judge is lap times, or crossing the finish line ahead of the field.

Visual Fields

Where you look determines nearly every aspect of your driving—speed, comfort, style, and safety. But it is important to use you eyes effectively to become a better driver and to go faster as well. Visual fields are one of the most important areas of attention for any competition driver. What you see determines how you implement and modify your game plan. If you fail to see something important, it can cause problems. In all forms of driving, knowing where to look and what to look for is crucial to both success and safety.

Visual fields are simply where you look and what the eyes are seeing. Most of the data gathered in a race car for decision-making is gathered visually. Your visual field could be the dashboard, down the track 300 yards, into a corner, at a billboard, or anywhere you look. A short visual field limits data gathering, and a long visual field promotes greater data intake.

The data you gather is needed to make decisions. "Where do I apply the brakes? When do I turn the steering wheel, and how much? What are the other cars doing?" Each of these questions and dozens of other are answered by visual data you take in while on the track. If the visual data you take in is faulty, inaccurate, or incomplete, the result will be lost time on the track and much greater risk. You'll either be too slow or too scared.

FOCAL POINTS

Your focal point determines what your visual field encompasses. Try this exercise right now. Focus on the

A driver needs to develop a visual field in which all driving and competition information is quickly processed. If your visual field is too large, you are receiving too much information and are not able to process all of it fast enough. If the visual field is too small, on-track events will happen too quickly. Bill Elliott and all other Winston Cup drivers have finely developed a visual field that works for them. *Nigel Kinrade*

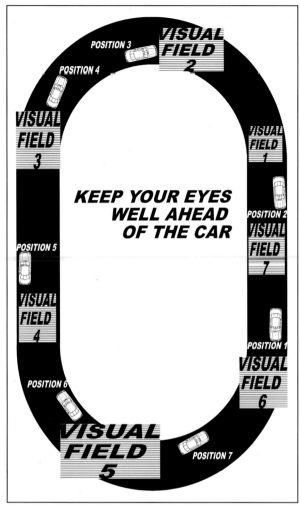

The goal is to always look down the track as far as possible or reasonable. This illustration shows the optimum area to be looking through at seven places around the track. Your eyes should make smooth transitions from one area to the next, rather than jump ahead. And your eyes should sweep through an area to gather all the pertinent data.

page you are now reading. Don't change your focal point, but notice what is in your peripheral visual field. What you see is limited, so the data you can gather from your visual field is limited. Now focus on an object several feet away. Do the same thing with your peripheral vision. You can take in more data. Try this on objects even farther away. As your focal point moves out away from you, your ability to gather important data improves. Within reason, the farther away your focal point is, the larger your visual field will be, and the more data you can take in with your eyes. What you focus your eyes on is very important.

THE CRYSTAL BALL

Your visual field is like a crystal ball. It allows you to take a look into the future. And the future can keep you ahead of the competition. For example, at 130 miles per hour, you are traveling at about 200 feet per second. If you look 200 feet ahead, you have one second to execute a move that will occur in 200 feet. But if you look at the bumper of the car just ahead, you have only 1/10 second look into the future.

With your visual field, you give yourself time for three important factors. First is the time you have to implement your plan. Second is the time you have to plan tactics based on the cars around you. Third is the most time you have to take evasive action in an emergency. You may have less time if the situation occurs within your visual field closer to you. Let's look at these more closely.

YOUR PLAN

Whether you realize it or not, you have a plan for getting around a race track. You must "plan" when to turn the steering wheel, when to brake, and when to use the throttle. Your visual field determines how far your plan reaches and how

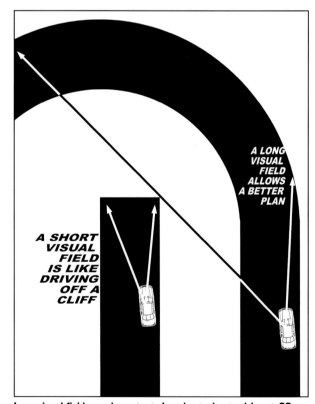

Long visual fields are important. Imagine trying to drive at 60 miles per hour on a road looking only out the side window.

Look at the driver's eyes. He is looking ahead and through the turn for the longest visual field possible.

The tape line across the windshield is a reference point that shows a driver where his eyes should be. Looking above the line allows a long, effective visual field. Below the line means the visual field is too close to the front of the car to allow for adequate time to execute a sound plan or react to changing on-track situations.

This series of photos on a test track is a good representation of how a visual field moves and what it looks like from inside a car. **(1)** After exiting a corner, the visual field should move to the end of the straight and take in as much of the next corner as possible. **(2)** The eye focus moves in as the braking zone is approached, but only for a second or two. **(3)** Early in the turn, the visual field moves through the midpoint of the turn, looking through to the exit as much as possible. **(4)** Exiting the turn requires the visual field to move down the straight to the next corner and its braking zone. **(5)** As braking begins, the visual field moves through the early part of the turn to the apex and beyond.

much time you have to implement the plan. If your visual field encompasses 100 feet in front of you, your plan for using the controls to position the car and control its speed extends 100 feet, and the time you have to implement the plan is determined by the speed of the vehicle. *For all practical purposes, your plan ends where your visual field ends.* To get through a corner effectively, you need a plan to get your car completely through a corner. And that requires a visual field that stretches through the corner. A big visual field will allow you to see the path you want to drive and will allow you to make smooth transitions on and off the controls. A short visual field, even if it shifts, does not allow you to see the big view. You are forced to make several smaller plans, leaving little time to implement the plan and requiring you to react to, rather than anticipate, situations. This forces more abrupt transitions and can cause you to lose speed.

TACTICS

Your visual field will affect your ability to create and implement tactics. The more you are forced to react to situations, the greater your *disadvantage* becomes. Larger visual fields allow you to anticipate tactical situations earlier in the majority of situations. If you count on reacting to situations, you will lose just about every time. If you give yourself time to anticipate the situation (attacking or defending), you will have a higher likelihood of success.

AVOIDING SITUATIONS AND CRASHES

A crash can happen directly in front of you, leaving no time to react and reducing your chances of avoidance. Your best chance for avoiding the situation is using a large visual field. The large visual field buys you time to avoid situations a little way down the track.

Visual fields should always be dynamic, always moving and changing. It is ineffective to focus on a marker or object 300 feet down the track, and maintain focus on that object until you pass it. To effectively use visual fields, you must constantly change them. Keep your eyes moving. For example, as you approach a corner, your eyes may sweep through the braking zone and through the corner to the exit. Then they may move back to your braking point and the path you plan to drive at the entry to

At the start/finish line, your view of the braking zone for Turn One, the entry to Turn One and the middle of Turns One and Two should look something like this.

At mid-turn, a short visual field will allow you to see how you're doing. Then move your eyes ahead as far as possible through the turn and onto the straight.

the turn. During this time, you may also glance at the mirror or use your peripheral vision to check on the position of other cars.

Visual priorities will change at different times, depending on your position on the track, the situation in a race, and other circumstances. It is best if you have an idea of where you need to shift your visual field at various points around the race track, or in various situations.

When entering a turn, the driver should look across the infield as much as possible to visually plan your line and exit acceleration.

All race tracks have reference points of some type. These points can be anything: marks on the race track, cracks, marks on the walls, poles, etc. Use reference points to help you create and maintain your plan. Be sure to use permanent markers, not ones that can move.

As you approach the braking area, you should look all the way through the braking zone into the corner, so that your plan is as complete as possible. Then shift your visual focus to the braking point and allow your eyes to follow your desired path through the braking zone. As the brakes are applied, your visual field should shift to the corner, so that you

have a clear mental picture of your desired path into and through the corner.

As you go into the corner, you should have already looked completely through the turn, then you can shorten your visual field for specific reference points. Once into the corner, your visual field should move to the exit.

You must see out of the corner as early as possible, so that you can unwind the steering and feed in throttle to maximize acceleration. This is probably the most important phase of the corner, and your visual focus is important. It is best to extend your visual field out of the corner as early as

These three views of the same turn show how a visual field should change. Exiting Turn Two, look all the way down the straight to see the big picture (1). Halfway down the straight, you need a slightly closer view of the upcoming corner (2). As you enter the turn, shorten the visual field to get a close-up look (3), then allow your eyes to look as far through the turn as possible.

possible. Once your path is determined on the exit, you can check the mirrors or gauges as you enter the straight.

INVISIBLE CORNERS

In many cases, especially on high-banked tracks, you will encounter a blind cornering situation. In these cases, regardless of radio communication from spotters, you need to have experience well below the limits of traction through those areas in order to drive them effectively. With experience, you will be able to get up to the limit. This process allows you to see "through" the blind spot as if it were not there. You are actually fooling your mind into believing that you actually see through the blind area. The risk is higher since you cannot see developing trouble, but you can drive to the limits using this technique. The key is to practice at low speed, gradually building speed as confidence and experience increase. With experience and confidence, you will start to approach the corner near or at the limits.

Developing Anticipation

On lap 17, you're in fourth place, running close to the leader. You are catching lapped traffic. As you approach Turn One, you see a situation forming that could cause you to change lines and reduce speed as you try to lap slower cars (Illustration 1). But you also know that an opportunity to pass may present itself. There are four cars ahead of the leader, all battling for position. Slower cars usually run in the low groove when being lapped, but as you approach Turn Four, the second car in the slow group dives under the first car, and makes the pass. You know that by Turn One the leader of the race will catch the slow group. The two lead cars in the slow group drive side-by-side down the front chute. The race leader drafts alongside the fourth car in the slow group, passing it going into Turn One. You are still in fourth place, but only three lengths behind the leader.

Going into Turn One, the two cars in front are side by side. The race leader is trying to get by the third position slower car underneath (Illustration 2). The two cars at the front of the group touch, causing the outside car to get out of shape and the inside car to slow down. The race leader and the third of the slower cars must decrease speed to avoid contact. The second and third place cars try to follow the race leader beneath the slower cars, so that they are now stuck below the third and fourth cars of the slow group (Illustration 3). For an instant, the cornering speed has dropped well below the limit for everyone in the group of eight cars, except you. You see the situation developing, so you stay high going

If a driver develops anticipation, he or she is better equipped to handle various racing situations, such as an opportunity to pass or to avoid a potential accident. Anticipation is important when negotiating traffic because a number of scenarios could develop, taking a driver out of the race. *Nigel Kinrade*

into Turn One. When the bottleneck occurs and speed drops, you have sufficient room and traction to stay up high in the turn and get by some cars on the outside. Through mid-turn, and into Turn Two, you squeeze by all of the slow cars. At the exit of Turn Two, the leader is able to go inside the slow traffic, still in the lead (Illustration 4). However, you have a better line off Turn Two, and are carrying more speed down the straight, giving you a clear shot at the lead going into Turn Three (Illustration 5).

Unlikely situation? Somewhat, but it does happen. It rarely occurs because most race drivers react to a developing situation. They do not *antici-pate* the potential situation, nor do they have a plan to make use of a situation like the one above, should it arise. The guys who make bonsai passes in traffic are often looked upon as aggressive and taking unnecessary risks. In reality, those drivers are using their ability to *anticipate* to their best advantage. By anticipating, the risks are minimized.

DEFINING ANTICIPATION

Webster's Dictionary says that to anticipate is to foresee or act in advance. Another definition says that it is the visualization of a future event. Think about those definitions for a minute. Looking forward and seeing a future event. Every second you are on the race track, you need to use anticipation to be fast, to plan passes and defense, and to race safely. Anticipation is looking into the future. Anticipation is recognizing clues that allow you to plan an action before the action is necessary. Anticipation is taking a look into the future by using the senses to make judgments based upon sensory inputs and past experiences.

When driving a race car, anticipation can be used in three ways. First, you can use anticipation to preplan the use of the car controls; and this affects speed and track position. The better you anticipate your own action, the closer to the limit you can consistently drive. Second, you can use anticipation to make an educated guess about the actions of other drivers. Finally, anticipation can be used to effectively avoid incidents and crashes on the race track.

LOOKING AHEAD

Looking ahead with a wide visual field is the essence of effective anticipation. As we have seen in the visual field chapter, your visual field determines how far into the future you can see. If your future is shorter than your reaction time, you stand little chance of avoiding bad situations or being able to take advantage of opportunities. Your visual field should encompass as much of the track as possible and should be constantly on the move. Mirrors should be included in the visual field. If you encounter a blind section of track, common on high-banked tracks, use prior knowledge of the terrain and your own experience to "see" through the blind area mentally. The clearer your mental image, the easier you can anticipate what is coming and incorporate accurate information from your spotters as part of your visual field plan.

STEERING

Anticipation is a great tool for managing steering inputs. When a driver makes a steering wheel movement based on reactions, the movement is usually abrupt. This can upset the balance of the car. Abrupt inputs may be unavoidable in emergencies, but they are unnecessary for normal steering wheel movements. Most drivers need only look ahead and plan their action to make a precise, smooth maneu-

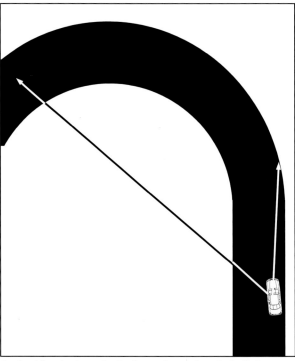

As the driver begins to brake, he or she needs to look all the way through the corner to the exit. The driver should be looking at the area between the arrows before entering the corner. The more information the driver is able to digest, the better the plan of action will be. In turn, the farther the driver looks down the track, the easier it will be to anticipate a crash or an opportunity to pass.

ver. The time to focus attention on steering is before you need to move the steering wheel. When approaching a turn, the eyes should be looking ahead to the point on the track where the car must be rotated into the turn. The eyes then move ahead through the turn as far as possible *before* the steering input is made. This gives you a clear picture of the path you want the car to follow through the turn. If the whole picture is not clear, the steering wheel movements will not be as smooth and precise as they should be. By finding your turn-in point and creating a mental path through the turn before taking steering action, a precise line can be driven smoothly. In addition, it can give you more attention to monitoring traction and traffic while in the corner.

BRAKING

As with steering, the driver's braking inputs should be anticipated to make them most effective. By finding the turn-in spot as you approach a corner *before* applying the brakes, you can sense speed and traction and have an improved feel for the exact location to apply the brakes and how hard the brakes must be applied. If you pick a braking point, you may not be able to slow the car at the best rate for the conditions existing at that moment. A driver should

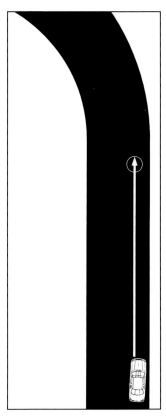

As the driver exits a turn, he or she needs to determine the braking point for the next turn. If the track does not have a braking marker, the driver should select a readily identifiable area of the track, such as a sign, a tire mark, or some other distinguishing feature.

use some of his attention on the straightaway, prior to applying the brakes to monitor traffic and sense speed and traction. This will give you important data concerning when and how firmly to apply the brakes. If you wait until you apply the brakes, your braking action is less likely to be smooth and efficient. It also reduces your ability to maintain consistency.

ACCELERATION

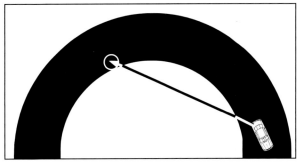

As the driver enters the turn, he or she needs to find an acceleration reference point. The goal is to find the earliest point where the car can accelerate out of the corner without spinning or losing traction. The driver will find that point past the apex of the turn. The illustration shows an arrow pointing to a possible acceleration reference point.

Acceleration requires the use of anticipation as well. Once the car is rotated into a turn, attention can easily shift to the exit of the corner. Where will you pick up the throttle? How much traction is available for acceleration? How quickly can you go to full throttle? By planning ahead, you will be able to have good data that will provide clues to help you get maximum acceleration exiting the comers.

STARTS AND RESTARTS

Anticipation is a great tool for planning starts and restarts. Knowing how a flagman will conduct a race start or restart can give you a distinct advantage over drivers who do not have that knowledge. Study what the starter does prior to a race start or restart. Also, know the local rules. And it's helpful to have a good idea how the drivers around you at the start will approach the green flag situation. When will they accelerate? Where will they go on the race track? How aggressive are they?

PASSING AND NEGOTIATING TRAFFIC

Like the scenario opening this chapter, passes can be planned by using anticipation. Knowing where other cars are on the track, judging how traffic situations may develop, and knowing where your car is in its performance envelope will add to your ability to make a clean pass. Knowing the possible reactions, the weak and strong points, and the skills of other drivers can also help you to anticipate the actions those drivers may undertake on the track. This can help you anticipate on-track situations, and effectively take advantage of them. It also helps to create a plan that allows you to take a variety of actions based on what you anticipate will happen. In other words, have an open mind about situations on the race track.

For example, if the traffic bottles up and speed is reduced, more options open up for lines through a corner. This can present many options that can allow passes where you could not ordinarily make them. Your plan should include looking for these options as you see a "traffic" situation begin to develop.

DEFENDING POSITION

When you are defending a position on the track, anticipation can be used to cover a passing move from an attacking driver. You can also plan your defensive actions in advance. Create a plan before a race that allows for a variety of scenarios. The broader the plan, and the more open you are to changing situations, the more easily you can anticipate situations and fend off attacks.

Included in the plan for defending position is how often, and where, you check your mirrors and what information you need from a spotter. Additionally, you need to know where you are strong and weak on the track before you get into a race situation. Attacks are easy to defend where you are strong but much more difficult where you are weak. Knowing the difference gives you more options for defense.

AVOIDING CRASHES

Ten laps into the main event, you are leading but being pressured by the second-place car. In three laps, you will encounter the first lapped traffic. You are already planning how to handle the traffic, and are paying as much attention as possible to the situation as it develops. Going into Turn Three, you plan to pass the first of the slower cars going into Turn One. As you brake going into Turn One, the last car in the line of traffic ahead of you dives low, trying to pass the car just ahead. You brake hard and try to get higher on the track to avoid contact when the second-place

car nails you in the rear bumper. Since you are moving high, with some steering lock to the right, the impact sends you spinning into the wall and out of the lead.

> **When a car crashes ahead of you, try to think where this car is going to go.**
>
> *–Jeff Burton*

The big question here is whether the following driver could have avoided hitting you. Mostly likely, the answer is yes. The trailing driver was not anticipating very well, so had no time to avoid the situation when it presented itself. He figures he "got caught up" in the situation; you figure he's a bonehead. But if he had looked ahead, he may have been able to avoid the incident. He was probably looking just beyond the front of the car instead of as far ahead as possible.

One of the most important uses of anticipation is avoiding crashes. Anticipation can help in several ways. Look ahead as far as possible. The sooner you see a situation develop on the track, the more time you have to react. Watch other cars for signs of problems. Water leaks, smoking exhaust, tire smoke, and so on, can each indicate a developing problem that could lead to an incident on the track.

Monitor the condition of your car. Is the water temperature climbing? Are there any other signs of impending failure? Are the brakes going away? Are you getting fatigued in the cockpit? Is the handling changing? Each of these factors could indicate an impending systems failure, which could cause a crash. Early detection can allow you to anticipate the situation, take early action to avoid the problem, or minimize its consequences.

ANTICIPATING POTENTIAL INCIDENTS

Another aspect of anticipation requires experience, judgment, and intense concentration. With astute observation and an educated guess, you can anticipate the actions of other drivers as they happen, or even before. For example, you are following another racer whom you have raced against for several seasons. You know that he lifts of the throttle a half a length earlier when coming up on slower traffic he is not familiar with. This can present an opportunity for you to pass when this situation occurs, especially if you can anticipate what the slower car may do as well.

Another example can save you from getting involved in a crash. You are following another driver closely. His car is getting more loose as the race progresses, but the driver doesn't compensate by slowing, changing lines or otherwise altering his technique. As the race progresses, you can bet that you will have an opportunity to pass, but if the situation gets any worse, the other driver is likely to stuff his ride in to the fence. By planning what you will do if the inevitable occurs, you greatly increase your chances to avoid his crash and make an easy pass.

USING ANTICIPATION TO GO FASTER

First and foremost, you should always look well ahead of where you are on the race track. As you set up the turn-in point of a corner, look all the way through the corner to the exit. This helps you "see" the path you want to drive. As you approach the braking area, you should find the spot where want to release the brakes before you apply them and anticipate the speed you want to be going at that point. Before you release the brake pedal completely, find the spot on the track where you plan to pick up the throttle. Before qualifying, close your eyes and visualize the path you want to drive, where you will brake, where you will apply the throttle, and how the car will feel. This will get you into a rhythm before you get on the track.

STRATEGIC ANTICIPATION

As a driver, you should study the racing styles of your chief competitors. Watch the hand movements of the driver ahead of you. You will see clues about what that driver may do.

Watch the attitude of the car ahead. Is its attitude changing? Is the car getting loose or pushing? Look as far down the track as possible at least twice a lap to see how traffic situations are developing. Watch your mirror as often as possible to see what is developing to the rear. Car placement of the following car can give you clues about what the following driver may try to do to pass you. In addition, watch the flagman and the fans in the stands for clues about on-track action.

Practice and develop your anticipation skills in your daily driving. Paying attention to the entire environment can offer important clues.

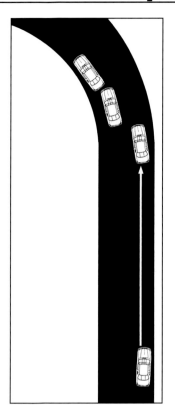

The driver should look as far ahead as possible and evaluate the traffic situation developing on the track. With this information, the driver can formulate the best passing plan and save time in the process.

PRACTICE EXERCISES

There are many ways to improve your anticipation skills. On the race track, pay attention to your own driving and plan ahead as much as possible. Watch what other drivers do when you are following them. You may anticipate their actions by watching what they do with the steering wheel. You can see the steering wheel move just before the car will change direction.

Similarly, watch the lead driver's eyes and head movements. A glance in the rearview mirror or to the side may tell you where the driver plans to go. By observing you can become more attuned to possible moves by other drivers nearly as soon as they are.

You can also practice these exercises during your everyday driving. Pay attention to what other drivers are doing. See if you can determine what actions they will take. You will quickly learn when someone plans to turn or stop without any signals. You can practice looking "through" other cars to the cars ahead to improve your anticipation and lengthen your lead time. Practice eye movements and try looking through corners, even if you cannot physically see through them. All of these exercises can improve your anticipation skills, and improved anticipation will make you a more effective, faster race driver.

EIGHT

Creating and Managing On-Track Priorities

A driver has a finite concentration capacity, and he or she must wisely spend the right amount of attention focused on the right aspects of driving. A successful circle track racer must define the priorities for qualifying and the race. He or she must be able to shift focus from one area of racing to another when necessary.

As you exit Turn Four on a qualifying lap, you feed in power smoothly. You unwind the steering as the throttle pedal opens wider. As you exit the turn, the car moves within 1 foot of the wall. You glance at the starter to confirm that you are getting the green flag. At the start/finish you look ahead into Turn One, mentally defining the braking zone and the point where you turn-in. As you approach the turn-in, you lift off the throttle smoothly as you apply the brakes. You sense traction as the car reaches its limits of adhesion. You then turn the steering so that the car can enter the turn. As you feed in steering lock, you lightly ease off the brakes, using as much tire traction as possible. At the same time you look through the turn, planning your exit from Turn Two.

Easing off the brakes at the same instant the car reaches peak cornering force, you glance at your turn

Dale Earnhardt won seven Winston Cup championships because he had the ability to efficiently manage on-track priorities and the many other facets of driving. In particular, he was able to concentrate on one particular task when necessary and could shift that focus to other areas. *Nigel Kinrade*

apex for reference. You immediately shift your eyes to the exit of Turn Two, while you pick up the throttle with your right foot. You have a clear mental "picture" of the path you're going to drive at the exit, and at the same instant you're sensing the traction of the tires while keeping the car right at the limits of lateral adhesion. In the next instant, you begin to unwind the steering as you apply the throttle, causing your car to accelerate. You are constantly monitoring traction so that more throttle can be applied, but you must also watch the path you are driving on to avoid the wall. Your exit path will take you right up to the wall under full power. As you exit the turn, you look down the back straight to get your reference points, and look beyond into Turn Three so that you can plan your path into the turn and plan your braking zone.

You listen for the engine revs and take a quick glance at the gauges. You then repeat the process of braking and turning as you approach Turn Three, following the same steps you used in turns One and Two.

You complete your lap, turning a very good lap time.

QUALIFYING

While on your qualifying lap in the above description, what actually occurred? What were you doing with your time and attention? A qualifying lap is the easiest scenario from a driving standpoint. All you have to do is manage your attention between traction and your desired path around the track, manage your visual field by looking at the most important areas of the track, then steer, brake, and accelerate. There is no traffic to monitor; no strategy to plan, no tire wear to monitor and no gauges to watch, at least not in any meaningful way, as there is during a race. And you only have to do this for about 18 seconds for a single lap. This part is easy, right?

During that 18 seconds, you shift priorities at least 30 times, visual fields at least 24 times, and attention as many as 100 times. You are managing different mental processes about 10 times each second. In a race, that number can double. During testing, it can triple. In each of these cases, you must drive the car precisely and consistently, while still managing other data. It is no wonder that paying attention to the wrong item

on the priority list at the wrong time can cause problems on the race track. And of course, this does not include extraneous data that enters the mind and has no importance to the job you are trying to accomplish.

PRIORITIES

At any given point on the race track, you must know what your priorities are or you will not be going as fast as you could. Priorities are constantly changing as locations change on the race track. They can change from lap to lap or corner to corner. In the qualifying example, you have three basic priorities:

- **Monitoring traction**
- **Controlling path**
- **Monitoring speed**

There are other priorities as well, like checking the starter or watching the gauges, but none of the others are ever the most important priority. One or more of the three listed above is always the most important priority during qualifying.

In a race, you can add the following to the three above:

- **Judging traffic**
- **Planning passes**
- **Planning defenses**
- **Managing tire condition**

You can add car setup to the list if pit stops are needed during the race. And during testing, not only must you drive the car to its limits, but you must also sense what the car is doing and analyze what is happening in order to make useful changes to the setup. It is very easy to experience sensory overload, which makes your job virtually impossible.

MANAGING YOUR DRIVING DUTIES

How can you manage to monitor traction, car condition, priorities, and visual fields effectively? Some drivers have a knack for this naturally. They always seem to know exactly where to look, where to place the car, when to use a control, and how much. Mental focus, priorities, and traction sensing are second nature. These drivers are usually calm, and they normally run up front. Other drivers always seem to be a step behind, never quite up to speed, just a tick off on timing, and often in the wrong place at the wrong time.

What's the difference between these drivers? Surprisingly little, and usually it's not driving skill. But if you sat in the grandstand and watched these drivers, you would sense a vast difference in skill levels. What is really happening is poor skills management. While the driver running in 12th place at your local track may never turn into a Jeff Gordon, that driver can get much closer with effective management of the skills listed previously.

MANAGING FOR FAST LAPS

For fast laps, the driver must manage three factors:

Monitoring Traction. To go fast consistently, you must focus a large portion of your attention on sensing tire traction. Something in the range of 60 percent of your attention is on traction while braking and turning into a corner. About 50 percent of your attention is on traction as you exit the corner, about 40 percent in mid-corner, and maybe only 15 percent on the straights after wheel spin is unlikely.

To learn sensing traction you need to program your on-board computer. You do this by practicing in a way that allows you to focus 100 percent of your attention on traction. A practice day on a skid pad or at your local track can help you tremendously. The more data points of experience you have, the more reliable your brain's "traction sampling" program becomes.

Keep in mind that your data acquisition system sensors are your hands, feet, seat of the pants, and your inner ear, where forces are most accurately sensed. Pay special attention to what these senses tell you while driving. Also remember that you control traction with three controls. You use the brakes and throttle to control speed and the steering to control paths. Speed and path directly affect

In a race, a driver needs to monitor traction, track position, speed, and traffic. In addition, passes for position, defending position and managing tires are also concerns. Throughout his career, Mark Martin has shown the ability to focus on any one of these areas while managing all the others in order to come up with a race win. *Nigel Kinrade*

traction. Change either, and you change how close to the limits of traction you are driving.

Controlling Path. Vehicle path is the easiest part of driving to monitor, since you basically will go where you look. The trick here is to look in the right place at any given point on the race track. If your arc through a corner uses 500 feet of track distance, you will have a very difficult time defining the arc you want to drive if your visual field extends only 250 feet. Two things happen if your visual field is too short.

First, it's nearly impossible to drive a precise line around the track or to find the points where you brake, turn, or accelerate if they are not on your "visual" map early enough. If your map ends too soon, you will get lost. If you take a trip from Daytona to Los Angeles, but your map and road signs end in Texas, you're going to spend a lot of your attention figuring out where to go.

When was the last time you drove looking about 10 feet in front of the car, or out the side window? How did that make you feel? Pretty damn uncomfortable, I hope. The second factor is time. If you look far enough ahead on the race track, you buy time. You're looking into the future. The farther ahead you look, the longer your glance into the future. The higher the speed, the more you need to look ahead. This gives you time to "plan" what you're going to do. It takes almost no attention to do what you are doing right now, if you have spent attention on planing. Looking ahead is how you do this.

In order to successfully negotiate a corner (or any part of the race track), your visual map must extend far enough ahead so that no more changes to the controls are needed up to that point. Otherwise, your plan ends before you've finished your job.

While the best path around the track is important, it is much more important to have a plan—including your visual field—of how you will drive the track. Keep your eyes ahead far enough and your plan will be effective, adapting to the fastest way around the track. Without a visual field large enough to allow a strong plan, you will spend far too much attention on controlling the car, and controlling your own anxiety.

If you use a long, effective visual field, you should never need to spend more than 30 percent of your attention on vehicle paths. If your visual field is too short, you may be spending up to 100 percent on paths, which is very ineffective.

Monitoring Speed. First, monitoring speed has absolutely nothing to do with reading the tach or a speedometer. Do that and you'll likely crash. Monitoring speed is a combination of visual perception and judgment. "When do I apply the brakes for this corner? How hard to apply the brake pedal?" This has little to do with miles per hour or rpm. It does, however, deal with time, speed, and distance judgments. Like monitoring traction, you must program your on-board computer with data, which comes from experience. You will learn by practicing "Gee, I could have waited a little longer to apply the brakes there" or "less pedal pressure would have worked better here" are statements you will be making to yourself. Experience will allow more accurate judgments of speed, time, and distance. Speed monitoring takes less attention in the turns and exiting the turns than it does on the straight as you approach your braking point. There it may take as much as 80 percent of your attention.

RACE PRIORITIES

During a race, you have many more "things" to do. Earlier we looked at additional factors you need to pay attention to during a race:

- **Judging traffic**
- **Planning passes**
- **Planning defenses**
- **Managing tire conditions**

Each of these requires considerable attention. Since driving fast can take 100 percent of your attention, where does the extra attention come from? It doesn't. Two factors must occur. First, you must have adequate experience at driving fast so that you spend less attention on driving and more on racing. Second, you must plan in advance how and when you will shift attention from driving fast to handling racing situations. It's not an easy task. Experience is helpful, but the key is to have a plan that allows you to focus on the most important priority. Often that priority is driving at the limit, at other times it's race tactics or strategy.

During a race, communicating with your crew chief and placing the car squarely in the pit box are also priorities that must be managed by the driver. A skilled driver, like Jeff Gordon, is able to effectively communicate with his team while juggling his other priorities. *Nigel Kinrade*

NONPRIORITIES

Part of a good racing game plan is to realize what things can interfere with your driving and racing. These things should become a priority *to avoid.* Here is a list—far from complete—to give you an idea of things to avoid:

- **Uncomfortable seating position**
- **Poor visibility**
- **Anger (and all distracting emotions)**
- **Self-criticism**
- **Dwelling on mistakes**
- **Any thoughts unrelated to doing your job**
- **What other drivers or teams are doing**

Priorities are important in all phases of life. On the race track, creating and managing priorities effectively is mandatory to achieve success.

Effective Radio Communication

Clear, concise radio communications are essential to success. At worst, radio communications can be distracting, confusing, and debilitating. At best, they can mean the difference between winning and losing.

"Drive 'er in deeper; you're losing time to the leader!"

"You're goin' in too high. The tires are gonna go away!"

"Go low in Turn Three."

Several years ago, when radios were first being used at the Saturday night racing level, I had little radio experience when I drove for a new car owner in a late-model sportsman on a half-mile oval. I made it through practice and qualifying, but the building frustration level grew beyond my tolerance point about 20 laps into a 100-lap feature. I was running midpack when the first caution hit at about lap 30. We did not need to make a pit stop to complete the race, but I came in anyway. When the car owner came over to the window, dropped the net and asked what was wrong I handed him the radio, which I really wanted to throw at him. I put the window net back in place and exited the pits in a less than subtle cloud of tire smoke. Naturally, I was the final car on the lead lap, and ended the race in midpack. Before I could "resign" as the driver, the car owner fired me. At least we agreed on something.

With more than a decade of hindsight, I handled the situation poorly, although I shouldn't have driven for this owner was a good move. But let's take a step

Radio communications during testing can help the driver better understand the car while helping the crew understand how the setup is working. Ricky Rudd uses lap time information from his pit crew to make driving changes. *Nigel Kinrade*

back to look at the real problem: poor communication on the radio. Let me warn a certain segment of car owners before you read any further—this chapter is from a driver's perspective, and I believe the driver should be the one driving the race car. For those who disagree, that is fine; at least consider this perspective.

A car owner or chief spotter who tries to drive a car over the radio turns the driver into a mechanical servo for a radio-controlled race car, and a very ineffective one at that. However, the radio is a phenomenal training tool for coaching a new driver, when it's done correctly. The race is not the time to coach a driver; that needs to happen at a racing school or during a test day.

In my situation, the car owner really wanted to be driving the race car and was trying to communicate every detail of how to drive the car. It drove me crazy. Events happen nearly instantaneously on the track and take far longer to describe and communicate over the radio. It was unbelievably distracting, making the information, even if it is good information, less than useful.

There are two ways to handle radio communication. The first gives the driver information to make a decision. The second tells the driver what to do or where to go on the race track. The first is much more effective while the second leaves doubt. Here are examples of each:

"Crash, Turn One, high groove." This is clear information allowing the driver to determine the course of action as his visual data adds to this information.

"Go low in Turn One." This is also concise, but the driver has no clue why to go low in Turn One. This creates a slight amount of confusion and uncertainty about the situation and slows the driver's ability to anticipate and react.

If you had any doubts, I prefer the first method because it defines the reason to take the high groove. The basis for the techniques used in this chapter come from the rationale that the driver needs information to help make decisions. To me, reacting to another's decision is much less effective. With that in mind, let's look at specifics about radio communication.

Clear, concise communication over the radio is intended to accomplish four specific goals:
- **Improve safety**
- **Gain a tactical advantage**
- **Key (remind) the driver**
- **Solve a setup problem**

Let's take a closer look at each of these in more detail.

SAFETY

In any form of racing, a driver has difficulty seeing everything going on around the car. This is even more so in the highly intense environment of the short track. While radios have not likely reduced the number of racing crashes, they have allowed for closer racing with a higher level of safety. And they certainly have reduced many unnecessary crashes.

> **The most important information from spotters is when a car is inside or outside or when there's been a wreck.**
>
> *–Jeff Gordon*

The first priority of spotter communication to the driver should be to tell the driver about impending trouble. This would include slowing cars, spins, crashes or debris on the track. In these cases a driver needs considerable information in a very short period of time. "Crash, front straight, low." The spotter tells the driver the whole story quickly and concisely. The word "crash" tells the driver what to look out for. "Front straight" tells the driver at what point on the track the problem is. "Low" tells the driver what portion of the track may be blocked. Unless the driver is within about 10 car lengths when the incident occurs, the driver has plenty of time to avoid the situation safely and cleanly. The longer the spotter takes to "spit out" the words, or the more words used, the closer the driver is to the situation, and the less time is left to make a decision.

If the spotter told the driver "Go high on the front straight," the driver would wonder what that means, since the driver normally goes high on the front straight. This statement is at best distracting and at worst confusing. The driver needs to know precisely what the problem is and where it occurred, so that a quick assessment can be made, followed by a decision, by the driver.

In many cases a driver can see things occurring that the spotter cannot, because the driver has the best perspective on the situation as it relates to the car and driver. Clear information over the radio combined with the visual data taken in by the driver gives the driver the maximum amount of information

> A spotter is very important. Having a good spotter can be the difference between winning and losing. But at the same time, the driver has to be the ultimate decision-maker on the racetrack.
>
> *–Jeff Gordon*

> Over the radio, you need to know from the spotter if there's a caution or a wreck, or what's happening with cars around you. From the crew chief, most of the information is when to pit and what adjustments need to be made during a stop.
>
> *–Jeff Gordon*

in the shortest time span possible. And this allows for the best decisions during the heat of battle.

Two factors are important. First, spoken communication must be clear and concise. Second, everyone on the radios, including spotter and driver, must know exactly what certain words and phrases mean. The words used are less important than the meaning. Everyone must be on the same page, so work out in advance the meanings of words and phrases.

The driver needs to know what the incident is, where it is on the track, and what groove may be

Roush Racing's Ted Musgrave confers with his crew chief during a qualifier for the 1995 Mountain Dew 500. It is important to have a clear set of rules and a defined use of speech before communicating over the radio. The crew chief and track spotters need to use clearly defined terms in short phrases, so the driver doesn't become confused or overwhelmed. *Nigel Kinrade*

obstructed by the incident. Here are words best used to describe an incident:
- **Spin**
- **Crash**
- **Car loose**
- **Slow car**
- **Debris**
- **Yellow flag**

Words to best describe locations around the track:
- **Turn One, Turn Two, Turn Three or Turn Four (or just the number)**
- **Kink**
- **Front straight or back straight**
- **Starter stand**
- **Pit entry**
- **Pit exit**

And here are words best used to describe what portion of the track may be obstructed:
- **Low or inside**
- **Middle**
- **High or outside**

If an information update is needed, it is usually because other cars get involved in the crash or a car hits the wall and slides across the track. The best way to describe this is:
- **Car sliding up the track (if moving from inside to outside)**
- **Car sliding down the track (if car moving from outside to inside)**
- **Another car involved**

Safety (Track Position—Other Cars)

While this category of communication is equally important for tactical reasons during a race, the safety factor is more important. When dicing for position on the track, visibility is often minimal for the driver, especially to the rear along the sides of the car. A spotter on the radio can more effectively see the big picture and can aid the driver in passing or being passed more safely. Anytime an overlap exists between two cars, a potential crash exists. An overlap condition occurs when two cars are side by side within 1 inch or less of each other. The driver needs to know if he is clear to the sides or if an overlap exists. This is most crucial when the overlap is very small, since that is the overlap most likely to cause a spin and crash. There are two distinct types of situations. The first is when the driver is passing another car. The second occurs when another car is attempting to overtake the driver.

> **What I never want to hear on the radio is, "Pick it up! Go faster! The leaders are two seconds behind you!" That's about the worst!**
>
> *–Jeff Gordon*

Passing and Being Passed

When passing, the driver knows the position of the car he is trying to overtake. What he does not know is when he has safely cleared the car he is overtaking. That is the spotter's most important job. The word most commonly used for that is "clear." Often, the car being overtaken will maintain an overlap and a counterattack. The driver needs to know what is happening. A phrase like "car still high" will work when the other car is holding position or "coming back low" or "attack low" works well in a counterattack situation.

If another car is attempting a pass, the driver needs to know early enough to mount a defense or to leave adequate room if being lapped. What the driver needs to know is what's happening (an attack or pass), what side (inside or outside) and how far back the approaching car is following. A phrase like "attack inside, two lengths" tells the driver that a car two lengths back is likely to try a pass to the inside. It may not be in the approaching corner, but it's coming. If the attempt is not initiated right away, then the driver needs updates so that he can easily keep track of the situation as it develops without spending too much time looking in the mirrors.

These overlap situations often cause crashes either because of poor communication between a spotter and a driver, obstructed views, or lack of response time. Spotters often take the rap for these problems, but it is always *the driver's* responsibility

to take appropriate action. It is important for the spotter to be positioned for the best view, but it is impossible to do that for every foot of the race track, so the driver must be the final decision-maker. Keeping communication short and clear will minimize problems, and is one key to success.

GAINING A TACTICAL ADVANTAGE

While most of the communication in the above section relating to passing and being passed is important tactical communication, there is another category of tactical information useful to the driver. Someone on the team should be assigned to watch other cars, especially cars leading your driver. This person does not need to be on a radio, but should pass along pertinent information to the spotter or crew chief, who can then pass it along to the driver. The most common situation occurs when another car is observed with a small handling problem that may cause the car to slow slightly or alter its line through one or more turns. This can create a tactical advantage if observed and used effectively.

For example, if you're in fourth position with 20 laps remaining, and the leader is picking up a push, you will be able to catch, and pass, the leader without pushing any harder and overdriving your tires. Then more attention can be paid to the second and third place cars. There are many situations like this, and keen observation and tactical planning can pay big dividends.

KEY (REMINDING) THE DRIVER

The most obvious time that the driver should be keyed for a situation on the track is for starts and restarts, or cautions. It is important to be precise and use words like *green, yellow,* or *caution.* Using the word *go* can be confusing since it sounds very much like *no.* Limiting the possibility of confusion is most helpful.

Often it is helpful to remind the driver of specific issues and situations. These can be unique to the driver, event, car, or the track, or they can be general reminders that allow the driver to focus on other more important matters. Here are some examples:

- **Cold tires (after a stop or a caution)**
- **Changing fuel load**
- **Overdriving the tires/conditions**
- **Being patient**
- **Staying calm**
- **Turning on cooling fans**
- **Reading temps and pressures**

Any reminder should be concise and preplanned, so everyone knows what is meant by the phrase used.

SOLVING PROBLEMS

In long races, or during practice and testing, solving handling and setup problems is important. In most cases, the driver should simply communicate what the car is doing, not offer the solution to the problem. When a driver offers solutions, attention is diverted from the driver's primary task, and the crew chief, to some degree, is taken out of the equation. This is the opposite of a car owner or crew chief trying to drive the car over the radio. The driver is less effective at solving setup problems over the radio than the crew chief. (The exception is the rare case in which the driver has considerable experience and the crew chief has little or none.) The driver needs to focus on driving and determining the nature of the problem.

What the driver should communicate to the crew chief is what the car is doing, how much, and where on the track. Here's an example. "It's pushing slightly going in, but OK everywhere else." This allows the crew chief, who has more time and attention to focus on problem solving, to determine the best solution.

If the driver says "put a turn in the right rear," the team's options are limited, as team members do not know what the problem is. If a driver is very experienced and understands setup and tuning, the crew chief may come on the radio, especially during a caution, and tell the driver the planned change. The driver may veto the plan or offer an alternative. This system can be very effective for problem solving during a long race or test session.

There are several logistical matters to keep in mind. Spotters should be positioned so that maximum track coverage is obtained with the fewest number of people. If more than one person communicates to the driver, establish a clear and rigid protocol for communication. Speak clearly and consistently.

Hearing two people trying to talk at the same time over the radio is very distracting and nearly impossible to decipher. If there are two spotters and a crew chief, only the crew chief addresses non-tactical or safety issues. One spotter covers and talks only from the starter's stand to the middle of the back straight and the other spotter covers the other half of the track. How the track and the communication are divided is much less important than being divided and everyone sticking to the plan.

It is best for spotters to be positioned as high as possible and outside the track, rather than in the infield. Key the mike before beginning to speak. If you start to talk before the radio kicks in, the first word or two will be lost, and if your communication is concise, important information is left out. In most communication, it is unnecessary for the driver to respond. Sometimes the driver can acknowledge a message with a click of the microphone key. Other times, a verbal response is needed. Work this out in advanced so everyone knows what to expect.

Have a contingency plan for radio malfunction or failure. Simple hand signals work well, and a pit board is needed to get info to the driver.

Keep in mind that like all aspects of racing, good communication, especially on the radio, takes work and practice. Use simple, understandable language that everyone understands; be concise and give information, not judgments, so that the appropriate person can make decisions. By following these suggestions, you can establish effective radio communication on your team. This will, in turn, improve the quality of your team's total effort and its on-track success rate.

Robert Yates Racing driver Dale Jarrett knows how to communicate vital information over the radio as a team member and a driver. He has coached several drivers and has called races for his son Jason, who runs in the ARCA series. *Nigel Kinrade*

Learning a New Racetrack and Qualifying

Going to a new race track is both fun and challenging. The first key to success is finding the fast way around the race track. There should be a procedure or method to learn it. When you go to a new track, there are several basic aspects to learn about the track. Once you find the pit area (entry and exit) and learn the basic configuration of the track. Note the location of the starter stand; the yellow lights or flag stations; the inside wall and any breaks in the wall; the pit entry and exit; and the locations of emergency and fire crew stations. Following are some tips to get fast, right off the trailer.

First, walk the track. You can often spot the "groove" when you walk the track, plus you get a feel for the racing surface. At that time, you should examine the banking. You need to pay attention to the banking angle because many tracks have inconsistent banking angles in the corners. The fastest line is usually found at the steepest banking angle on the race track.

When you're new to the track, talk to the other drivers. Often, you can learn a lot from the veterans,

The driver must conscientiously learn the track and build speed. First, the driver needs to increase exit speed, which is fundamental for setting a fast lap. Second, maintaining the highest cornering speed is important. Third, the driver needs to learn how to enter the corner as fast as possible without losing time.

These photos show the same corner. Good reference points include the building, the end of the row of signs, and the marks on the wall. Poor reference points would include palm trees and poles. The lines on the track surface make good lateral position references.

> **The most important thing a new race driver needs to learn is how to earn the respect of the other drivers.**
>
> *–Jeff Gordon*

saving yourself track time by learning things yourself. If you're a rookie and pose little or no threat, the information is probably accurate. If you're a fast veteran, competing drivers may give you false information, so be careful. You should ask how track conditions change throughout the day and night. The track crew or promoter will usually give you good advice.

Another important tool to use when learning a track is to draw a map, record reference points, de-

The Irwindale Speedway sign on the wall and the American flag are good reference points.

> You try to be aware of every track you go to and the configuration and what the things are that you can hit. So if something does happen, you're aware of where you're at on the track. You might have to do something different at a different track.
>
> *–Terry Labonte*

The driver should study banking angles. While hard to see in the photo, this track has three banking angles, with the steepest at the top. That will influence the way you drive the track and is an important part of learning a new track.

celeration areas, rough spots in the surface, and any other observations you have. This helps to solidify your thoughts and ideas and is invaluable when you run on the track. At that time, you should find your reference points by examining the track and incorporating them in your track map. They will be helpful. Reference points should be stationary and permanent.

You should watch competing cars on the track. Pay special attention to the fastest local drivers during practice. That should give you clues to the fast line around the track. A driver should learn a new track by gradually increasing speed and driving comfortably. Don't try to set a lap record the first time out. Work on driving a good line and dri-

The track entry gate and the blank sign are good reference points. Using a specific sign by names can take too long to be useful. You can use signs by color, however.

The track exit gate and the ball-shaped sign are both good references.

The tall power pole is a good reference exiting the previous corner, and the dashed lines provide lateral position references.

The pit entry gate, the last billboard, and the Winston racing series sign are good reference points.

The inside berm is good marker, and one you can feel if you get too close.

ve as smoothly as possible. You should pick up your brake, turn-in, and acceleration points. The speed will come if you focus on driving the track precisely and smoothly.

Once you have watched the fastest drivers, you should follow the fast drivers in practice. You can gain knowledge by following fast drivers from the new track, but once again, be careful. They may know you're behind them and show you the wrong line. Use your own judgment and follow your instincts.

FIRST PRIORITY

In order to go fast, your first priority is to work on the corner exit. Find a line that lets you get off the corner with the earliest, hardest acceleration possible *without* spinning the tires. Wheel spin is slow on asphalt.

SECOND PRIORITY

Corner speed is your second priority. Some tracks and some cars need momentum for fast laps. Others are less critical in this area. Work on speed through the corner and adjust accordingly so power can be applied as early as possible.

THIRD PRIORITY

The third and final priority is getting into the corner. Little speed will be found here, but much can be lost.

There are other aspects to consider. If passing is part of your plan, and it should be, find other lines into and off the corners and alternate grooves through the turns. The driver will find out what it's like in "no man's land," and this will give you a good feel for making passes during the heat of battle. By watching other races, you can learn about other racers and their technique, which can help in passing and traffic situations. Mental practice is a great way to get more "seat time" when you're out of the car. Use a stopwatch to time your mental laps and focus on driving smoothly. The more clearly you have your mental picture developed, the easier it will be to drive the track quickly.

A new driver should understand the qualifying procedures. Different tracks have different procedures for qualifying. Some have single laps, while others have two laps. Know the ropes and be sure to know were the timing lights are positioned. In addition, you should familiarize yourself with the start and restart rules. Starts and restarts are very important. Know how the starter operates. Watch races you're not in and study the starter.

QUALIFYING

You're in line for qualifying. You were fast in practice, but you've never been really good at qualifying. You know that less than 0.7 second will separate the entire field. You need a good lap to

The patches on and next to the curb are good inside references, allowing you to check on your position. The light tower and the announcer's booth at the top of the grandstands are also good distant references.

The patch protruding from the curb is a good mark. Stand-alone signs, like the ones on the left of this photo, are also good.

make the show and an even better lap to avoid second-round qualifying. The pressure is intense. You're next to go and the engine is warming up. It's hard to focus on driving because you're worried about the outcome. The NASCAR official waves you out for your run. You have one warm-up lap and two green flag laps before the checker waves.

You begin to relax as you accelerate out of the pit lane onto the track surface. You work the car hard on the warm-up lap to put heat into the tires. The car feels good. You get a good run off Turn Four as you come down for the green flag. You drive her hard into Turn One, but not too hard. The tires get side bite and you pick up the throttle, getting a good run off Turn Two and down the back straight. You get into Three smoothly, but exiting Four you're too hard on the gas and the rear tires spin as the car pitches slightly sideways. Not a big problem, but costs you time on both laps because that run of Turn Four completes your first lap but also starts your second lap.

The rest of the lap goes well, but the two-tenths that bobble cost you moves you back 15

> **Qualifying is more important than it ever has been. Passing is extremely hard on a lot of tracks. Pit stalls on pits stops are important, so that makes qualifying more important.**
>
> *–Jeff Gordon*

spots on the starting grid. Where you could have been in the top 10, you're now barely able to avoid second-round qualifying.

What went wrong? Qualifying is the most difficult aspect of driving race cars for most competitors. You have to get the tires up to optimum operating temperature, the setup is crucial, you have no time to get into a rhythm and you have a lot of pressure. And everybody is watching you! It's a tough deal for all drivers, but some are much better than others. Most often the key factor is mental preparation. Different drivers have different approaches, but some form of preparation is needed for a successful qualifying effort.

First, a driver and team must have a precise plan for the qualifying run. How hot do the tires need to be? How many laps are green, one or two? How many warm-up laps will you get? What's the optimum line for a two-lap run? Each of these issues must be part of the qualifying plan. The team must address each factor to stand a chance of putting in a successful run.

> On a warm-up lap before qualifying, I generally try to get heat in the tires by getting up to speed quickly. I drag the brakes, and instead of coming right out and going to the top of the track, I stay on the bottom through the turns, making a sharper angle and working the tires harder to get some heat in the tires.
>
> *–Ricky Rudd*

Most tracks require as much heat as possible in the tires. The superspeedways are sometimes an exception. Many drivers heat the tires ineffectively during the warm-up lap. Swerving the car to heat the tires is not the best way. Swerving is great for cleaning the tires, but most often, sticker tires are used for qualifying and need no cleaning. And if scrubbed tires are used, they should already be clean. The best way to heat tires is by hard acceleration, braking, and cornering. Hard acceleration out of the pits heats the rear tires while overly hard braking into the first corner will get more heat in to the front tires. Slightly overdriving the middle of the corner will heat all of the tires. The driver may need to alter the technique to get the tires hot during the warm-up lap, or even during the first green flag lap. Once the tires are hot, the driver must revert to a smoother, more precise driving style.

Here are some tips for effective qualifying:
- **Know the qualifying procedure—how many hot laps and how many warm-up laps.**
- **Get in the car early to begin focusing.**
- **Get heat in the tires quickly, especially on a cold track.**
- **With two laps, get a good, clean run on lap 1 and try pushing more on lap 2.**
- **On a two-lap run, be very careful exiting Turn Four because a mistake will affect both laps.**

**TURN 4
TWO LAP
QUALIFYING
END OF LAP 1**

Exiting Turn Four at the end of lap 1 on a two-lap qualifying run is the worst place to make a mistake. This part of the track affects both lap times, so be conservative here.

> On the warm-up lap before qualifying, you get your speed up quickly.
>
> *–Terry Labonte*

- **Be as smooth as possible with the controls.**
- **Be careful not to overdrive the corner entry and scrub speed.**
- **Corner exit wheelspin can kill straightaway speed, so ease on the throttle.**
- **Track conditions change during qualifying so take what the track can give and don't try to get too much from the car.**
- **Remember to stay ahead of the car with long visual fields.**

> Sometimes the line for qualifying is the same for the race, but often the qualifying line will be different.
>
> *–Terry Labonte*

> You drive a lot harder during qualifying because your tires are fresh, and you usually have more downforce.
>
> *–Jeff Burton*

THE MENTAL SIDE OF QUALIFYING

The biggest factor for a good qualifying run is all mental. Most professional drivers have the necessary skills to run one or more very quick laps during practice or a race. So speed is not the problem. Most drivers in oval track qualifying find it difficult getting into a rhythm. Additionally, when a driver considers himself a mediocre or poor qualifier, that lack of confidence makes it difficult to focus on the job that must be done.

To become a top-notch qualifier, a driver must first learn to focus completely on the job of qualifying. A driver must not allow extraneous thoughts to change the focus to a possible negative outcome. Then the driver must find a way to get into a rhythm very quickly.

A few drivers have a knack for getting up to speed quickly. Most do not. One trick some drivers use is called visualization. Visualization, in this case, is nothing more than running mental practice laps. The driver can "see" the track, "hear" the car, and feel the sensations of driving the course. The more vivid the mental image, the better it works. In some cases, drivers will practice visualizing laps before an event and actually time laps with a stopwatch. It is surprising how realistic the lap times are when this is done.

When you have only one lap to get up to speed, the driver feels pressure because it is very hard to be at the peak with little warm-up time. To utilize visualization effectively for qualifying, a driver will get into the race car early, strap in, and put on the helmet. The driver closes his eyes and starts running laps mentally. From exiting the pit lane to seeing the green flag wave, the driver must feel that feeling of actually being on the track. Being able to "see" the stands, the walls and the gauges, to "feel" the acceleration and braking allows the driver to experience the mental sensations of driving and fall into a natural rhythm before hitting the track for real. If it takes a driver 10 laps to "get comfortable," the driver must complete at least 10 laps before he gets the call to start a qualifying run. The better the driver does this, the more real the experience, and the better the qualifying effort.

There is an important added benefit to this. By focusing concentration 100 percent on the mental practice laps, the driver has no time or concentration available to focus on the desired outcome or the fear that the desired outcome will not occur. This makes getting "psyched out" less likely, and makes staying focused on the job easier.

Other drivers use other techniques to get into the groove. Some will go through a mental checklist; others have the spotters or crew chief talk them around the track, often using key words that help the driver stay focused and calm. The important thing for the driver is to find something that is effective, race after race.

So the next time you watch a race and see a driver taking a nap before qualifying, it is likely that the driver's eyes are closed while running mental laps before hitting the race track. One the other hand, if the driver is really asleep, that is one cool customer.

Planning Race Strategy and Tactics

A race strategy provides an overall plan for key events in a race. This defines the pace the driver will run at various stages, the best places to pass most drivers, when to change lines and a multitude of other factors. Tactics are a plan of action for a specific situation.

On lap 52 of a 100-lapper, you're in second place when a yellow flag flies. You do not need to fuel to finish the race, but right side tires would give you a shot at winning. You radio your crew, but they are not prepared and the leader dives onto pit lane at the last second. You cannot react quickly enough and miss the pit entrance. Now you have no choice but to stay out. The good news is you have the lead. The bad news is that your tires will go off in about 40 laps. Not only do you lose the lead, but three other cars get by you, all of whom pitted for right side rubber back on lap 52.

Strategy is the creation of a plan before an event begins. Tactics is the implementation of that plan during the event. In the opening scenario, there was no plan and hence no strategy. And without a solid strategy, tactics are hit and miss. In this case, they missed, and it cost the team a race win.

In the above scenario, two important strategic elements were missed. First was a pit stop strategy. Second was a tire management strategy. Without a solid strategy beforehand, a tactical opportunity was missed due to indecision and some confusion. In the

Teams and drivers take various approaches to race strategy and tactics. While a well-defined race strategy may be in place before the green flag drops, accidents and unforeseen changes in track position may alter the race strategy. Here, Dale Jarrett reviews records and discusses race strategy with crew chief Todd Parrott. *Nigel Kinrade*

above example, the team should have developed a tire management and pit stop strategy something like this. "We know that after 40 or 50 laps, the tires are a half-second slower. If we get a caution near mid-race, we need to consider pitting for right side tires. We also know that we can run with the fastest cars for 100 laps if everyone stays on the same tires they started with, possibly even having an advantage over many of the teams. If we are in the top five or six cars and the leaders pit under caution, we should also. If they stay out, we should stay out too. But if we are in the last half of the field and the leaders pit, we will probably benefit more from staying out to gain track position. But if the leaders stay out during the caution and we are near the back, pitting for right side tires will cost little in track position and allow us to run faster and move up through the field."

> **Team leadership is very important to success on the race track. A good leader means you're well prepared when you get to the track, and you'll usually have a good week then. Having the right people and chemistry on the team is real important.**
>
> –Terry Labonte

Here is a very solid strategy that allows for several scenarios. The tactics, when in second place with a caution on lap 52 would be easy. The crew would radio the driver as soon as the caution flew (or even before) to follow the leader. Stay out if the driver stays out, pit if the driver pits. The other front-running cars will follow as well, unless they have chosen a weak strategy.

TEST

To develop a sound strategy, you need to find answers to several crucial questions. Testing is the most efficient way to find those answers. You need to determine fuel mileage during green flag runs and fuel mileage during caution periods. In addition, the driver should log lap times over the duration of a race length run when driven at 100 percent of the driver's ability. Typically, the lap times increase and the driver slows down in the later stages of a race. Likewise, the driver should log a

> **A strategy develops as the race goes on. Are we going to change two tires to four tires? For those strategies, you have to rely on the crew chief.**
>
> –Ricky Rudd

race length stint at 90 percent and then 80 percent of ability. After a driver has performed these three tests and recorded the data, the driver should determine the lower average lap time over a race length. You should discover at what stages of the race the tires fade and lap times lengthen. And you should be able to formulate a plan to vary the pace. For example, you might find out it is best to run 80 percent for the first half of the race, 90 percent up to three quarters of the distance, and 100 percent for the remaining quarter. In addition, you should learn what alternate lines allow for a faster overall pace and if alternate lines increase or reduce tire wear.

Answer these questions and you will have a clear picture of the strategy you need to create before a race. Then tactical situations will allow you to implement the strategy quickly and effectively. Write out your strategic plan, then summarize it with the key points and post it for the crew, but keep other teams from seeing your plan. Make sure every member of the team is dialed-in and prepared to take action as tactical situations unfold. Then opportunities to win or finish up front will not be lost like the situation opening this chapter. Winning races and championships requires sound strategic planning and rapid, concise implementation of tactics.

> **Tactical decisions are usually made by the crew chief. Sometimes he'll radio to the crew guys in the pits or to me, but he may have a better view of what's unfolding than I do.**
>
> –Terry Labonte

ELEMENTS OF AN EFFECTIVE STRATEGY

It should be obvious that a well-planned strategy makes tactical decisions easy and nearly instantaneous. Here are the areas that need strategic planning:

- Pit stops
- Tire management
- Fuel management
- Qualifying
- Race starts and restarts
- Pace at given times through the race
- Track position

PLANNING A STRATEGY

To plan a strategy you need to know the following:
- Fuel mileage
- The rate tires fade at a given lap time
- The best pace for the tires so that the fastest average lap times for the entire race are attained
- Rival drivers' tire management
- Weather forecast
- How other teams plan strategies
- How other drivers handle traffic
- Early and late race track position
- How traction changes as the race progresses
- How the groove moves during the course of the race
- How track temperature affects handling
- How the car and driver work in traffic
- How other drivers handle defending position
- How other drivers attack for position
- The actual time needed for a pit stop, including slowing, accelerating, and speed limits
- Where the starter will wave the green for a race start or restart

> **You really pay attention to what your car is doing and how it's handling before a pit stop, and relay that information to the crew chief.**
>
> *–Jeff Burton*

TACTICAL SITUATIONS

Tactics are more dynamic. Tactics take a strategic plan and put it into action. The current situation at a given moment will dictate the tactical move at that moment. As in our opening scenario, the strategy allowed for different decisions based on the tactical situation as it unfolds. You know certain things will occur during a race, like a caution. Your strategy will tell you what is best for you to do when certain tactical situations occur, like a yellow flag. Without the strategic plan, tactics won't work effectively. Here are several tactical situations or opportunities that need to be addressed in a strategic plan:

> **Tactical decisions are usually made by the crew chief. Sometimes he'll radio to the crew guys in the pits or to me, but he may have a better view of what's unfolding than I do.**
>
> *–Terry Labonte*

- Caution flag
- Laps remaining when a caution or other situation occurs
- Number of caution periods and laps relative to tire and fuel management
- Track position near the end of the race
- Traffic
- The position of following cars and their distance behind
- The racing profile of following drivers
- The position of leading cars and their distance ahead
- The racing profile of drivers ahead
- Changing track conditions
- Tire condition as the race nears completion
- Lap times
- Lap times of other cars
- Time limits or curfews
- Changing weather conditions

KEEP EXTENSIVE NOTES

In order to improve as a driver, you must build a solid foundation of information. A driver should log any pertinent information on driving techniques, driving problems, and track conditions in a notebook. Most importantly, you should keep records on your driving and your lap times. Thus, a driver can examine and reflect on driving a particular track, look at the technique being used in a particular section, and look for a possible way to pick up more speed. If a driving problem arises, the driver can identify the problem and work with the team or other trusted drivers to find a solution. Remember, before you can find the correct solution, the problem has to be accurately identified. If you have not correctly identified the problem, your solution will be incorrect. You should define the lines, braking points, and steering points you are using and write down a plan for making changes. In the next practice session, put your plan into use and record the results. In addition to driving technique, you should take notes on car setup, tire wear, fuel mileage, weather conditions, track conditions, other drivers and teams, and anything that is relevant.

TWELVE

Race Starts and Restarts

Race starts and restarts typically are the most dangerous times of the race. A sound plan, formulated according to the track configuration, conditions, car position, and the other drivers, is essential to capitalize on opportunities and safely avoid any accidents.

You're on the pole when the starter gives the signal for one lap before the green flag. You stay in the middle of the track, with the outside car right alongside. On the backstraight, the yellow light goes off. You hold position and keep the engine right at the threshold of the powerband. In the middle of Turn Three, you begin to accelerate in the low groove, but the outside car has moved up higher on the track and is 5 feet ahead. Entering Turn Four, you are on full power as the green light comes on. Approaching Turn One, the outside car blows by you and takes the lead. What happened?

Short of a car problem or a jumped start, the car on the pole should always have the advantage at the start of a race. In the above situation, the driver poorly positioned his car on the track, giving the outside car the best opportunity for accelerating off Turn Four early, and the best braking line into Turn One. The pole car has a big advantage because that driver controls the most important factors for the start: speed and track position. The only way to lose the lead starting from the pole is to give up position or start at an ineffective speed for your car.

Bobby Labonte is on the pole; Jeff Gordon is on the outside of row one, and behind them on row two are Tony Stewart and Dale Earnhardt. With the exception of Stewart, these Winston Cup stars have raced each other for nearly a decade. They know what to expect from one another, and thus, they devise a start plan according to the racers around them. *Nigel Kinrade*

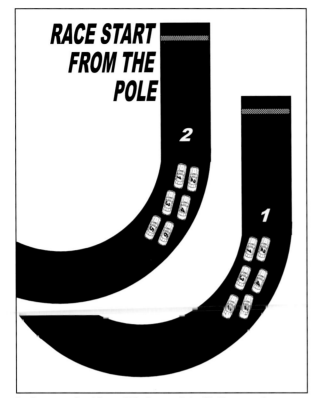

RACE START FROM THE POLE

In view one, the driver of No.1 moved the No.2 car to the outside in order to gain an advantage at the start. In view two, the driver of No.1 stayed too low exiting Turn 4 and allowed the No.2 car to gain an advantage at the green flag.

When you start on the pole, you set the pace. What is the best speed? Simply stated, the optimum speed to start is the speed where you have the best acceleration. Systematical acceleration testing or looking at dyno sheets will tell you what the best engine rpm is for peak acceleration. The heart of the torque curve is the right rpm. Too slow and the car will bog a little. Too fast and the power curve flattens out too soon—though too fast is much better than too slow.

However, you should be cautious. Abrupt acceleration from low speed can cause wheel spin, which kills acceleration. The tighter the track, the

> **With the amount of downforce on today's Winston Cup car and the quality of Goodyear tires, you've got to go pretty hard right from the start and make them last as long as you can.**
>
> *–Jeff Gordon*

> **The way you position yourself for a restart could be a little bit different for some tracks. You try to make sure you can accelerate with the cars ahead. Since there's no passing before the start/finish line, you can't pass after that at most tracks anyway. It's mostly getting off to a clean start.**
>
> *–Terry Labonte*

more likely wheel spin will hurt acceleration. It is crucial to apply the throttle smoothly to avoid this because abrupt throttle applications will induce wheel-spin, causing the car to oversteer.

TRACK POSITION

Even more important than pace is the lateral position of your car on the race track. From the pole, you can position your car anywhere, as long as you leave room for the outside car. The goal is to position the car so that you get the best acceleration run out of Turn Four. *You* want your line to be as straight as possible, with minimum steering-lock applied as you begin to accelerate when the green comes out.

In most cases, the best position is high on the race track. A common mistake is positioning the car too low on the back straight and going into Turn Three before the green flag. This allows the outside car to have the optimum position for acceleration. Keep in mind, the tighter you turn, the more likely wheel-spin will occur. Even on a speedway where wheel-spin is unlikely, a tighter turn will scrub speed and slow acceleration.

When you are high on the track between turns Three and Four you can unwind the steering wheel to get the best acceleration out of Turn Four. As you accelerate, let your car come as high as possible to the outside, leaving racing room for the outside car. As you approach Turn One, stay high under braking if the outside car is still next to you. You want to keep your optimum line into Turn One. Carry the outside car high again if necessary. Then you have the advantage exiting Turn Two.

Starting from the Outside of Row One

If you are on the outside of row one, you want to try to force the pole car to a low line on the track, allowing you to have the best run off Turn Four. Every advantage the pole car gains leaves you at a disadvantage. Just like the pole car, you want to have the best line for peak acceleration. Additionally, you also want to start at the best rpm for your car. Sometimes, the outside car can force the pace if the pole car is too slow. Easing ahead of the pole car often causes the pole car to pick up the pace. You also want to try to start a little ahead of the pole car if you can. This mostly depends on the starter. Some starters will throw the green even if the outside car is a few feet ahead.

Starting Behind the Front Row

Many drivers will leave a gap to the car ahead attempting to jump the green and gain an accelera-tion advantage as the flag drops. Perfectly timed, this strategy can work. Mistimed, you've blown it. If you mistime the green and have to back off, you will lose several positions. If you drop back too far, you leave a gap for another car to fill. This type of start is a high risk.

To make the best start from behind the front row, the driver should stay close to the cars ahead.

> Before every race, I stretch and take a lot of deep breaths trying to get as much oxygen to the brain as possible. This helps maintain concentration, but your experience and talent as a race car driver is key to how you focus on the track.
>
> –Jeff Gordon

In view 1, the driver of No. 1 is low on the track coming to the start. The No. 2 car is in a better position to accelerate hard. In view 2, the No.1 car has moved up the track coming to the start and is taking a straighter line for better acceleration. In this situation, it will be very hard for No. 2 to get a jump on the pole car.

Most drivers run the start strategy through their minds as they wait for the warm up lap. As the start nears, most drivers intensify their focus on the upcoming race. Bill Elliott and a crew member prepare for the start of the 2000 Brickyard 400, while Richard Childress and Dale Earnhardt finalize their plans as well. *Paul Johnson/Speed Sports Photography*

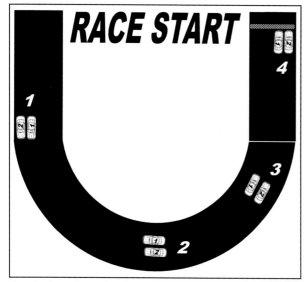

Here is the optimum line for the pole car (No. 1) to maintain the advantage coming to the start. Keeping high and forcing the outside car higher gives the pole car the best shot at the start.

If the car in front botches the start and driver behind is watching that car, the following car will botch the start as well. As soon as the green comes out, look for holes; they will appear, so be ready to take advantage.

Starting from the Inside Row

If you start from the inside, you want to follow the same guidelines as the pole car. Work the car above you so that your exit line from Turn Four is as straight as possible for maximum acceleration and minimal wheel-spin. Try to stay as high as possible; you can always find a hole to the inside. As with the pole car, watch for the car behind you to try to get inside into Turn One.

Starting from the Outside Row

The outside row has the advantage of a better, straighter line exiting Turn Four and entering Turn One. Because many of the inside row cars will move down in an attempt to pass going into Turn One, you should have some good opportunities to pass on the outside if a log jam occurs into Turn One. You also have a better exit line from Turn Two, so you can use that to your advantage into Turn Three on the first lap or two.

READING THE STARTER

The key to a good start is knowing the characteristics of the starter. Will the starter throw the green on the front straight, exiting Turn Four, or between Turns Three and Four? Will the green flag come out if the front three rows are ragged? Can you jump the start from the outside? Will the green flag fly if the rows are not straight? How likely is an aborted start if any of these situations occur? Knowing the answers to these questions, and others, can allow you to create an effective starting strategy based on the style of the starter. The

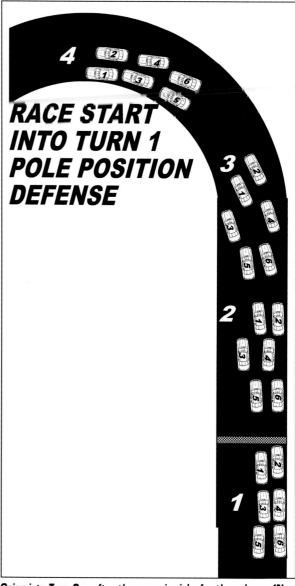

Going into Turn One after the green is risky for the pole car (No. 1). It will come under attack from the outside front row (No. 2) and the inside of row 2 (No. 3). If the pole car turns in too early, the No. 2 car will get by on the outside. If No. 1 turns in too late, the No. 3 car will get by underneath. In this scenario, the No. 1 car is taking a slightly early turn-in to fend off the No. 3 car, because the No. 2 car is less of a threat.

starter will dictate what you can and cannot manage at the start.

A spotter providing key information on the radio can be a big asset for the start. The spotter should know exactly when the green light comes on or the flag flies. Does the starter raise or drop the flag first? Does the green light come on before or after the flag drops? The spotter needs to know the answers. And when the green does fly, the spotter should inform the driver with a simple "Green!" A "Go!" or some other phrase could confuse the driver.

THE STARTING PLAN

Creating a strategy prior to the start will help you focus on the priorities. The plan should be created after you know your starting position. It should address all of the issues above and include options, because starts rarely work out the way you plan.

RACE START INTO TURN 1 ATTACK FROM OUTSIDE FRONT ROW

In this scenario, the No. 2 car gains an advantage going into Turn One because the No. 1 car turned in too early (2). At view 3, the No. 2 turns down hard forcing No. 1 to run too low. By view 4, the No. 2 car has a clear advantage and the No. 4 car is in position to attack going into the next turn.

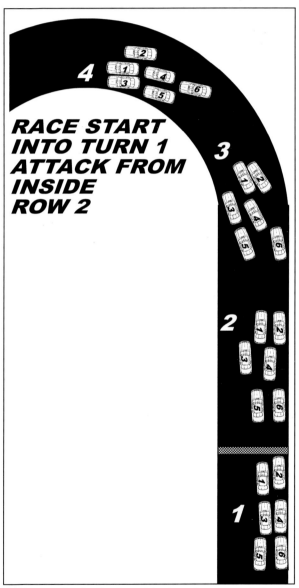

RACE START INTO TURN 1 ATTACK FROM INSIDE ROW 2

In this scenario, the No. 1 car defends against an attack from the outside front row (view 1), turning in too late (view 2) to defend against No. 3. In view 3, the No. 3 car has made a good move to the inside, forcing the No. 1 to stay too high. At view 4, the No. 3 car is in position to pass on the next straight, and the No. 2 car is under attack from No. 4 and could even get passed by No. 6 on the next straight.

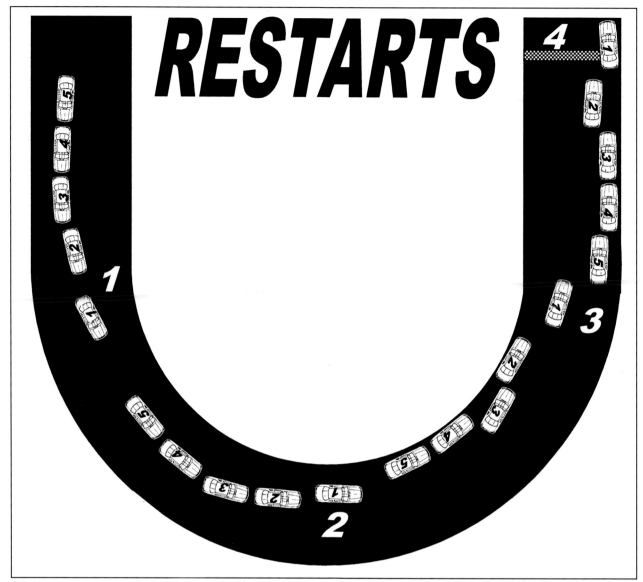

This restart scenario shows the leader (No. 1) taking a very late apex line to the exit of turn 4. At position 2, the No. 1 car can accelerate at full throttle and make it nearly impossible for following cars to get a run. If the leader took a normal line, this advantage would be reduced.

> **Before the green flag at the start of the race, you try to get heat in your tires and get the air pressure built up.**
>
> *–Terry Labonte*

Be ready for anything, especially evasive maneuvering. Keep the plan as simple as possible, because simple plans are the most effective.

The race start is the most challenging and enjoyable part of the event. A sound strategy will make the start even more enjoyable, possibly gaining you a spot or two on the field.

RESTARTS

Nearly everything that applies to starts works for restarts. The major difference is that restarts are in

> **On a restart with lapped cars ahead of you, you try to get by them as fast as you can. The leader has a clear track and will be putting a lot of distance between you and them, so you try to get by the lapped cars as quick as you can.**
>
> *–Terry Labonte*

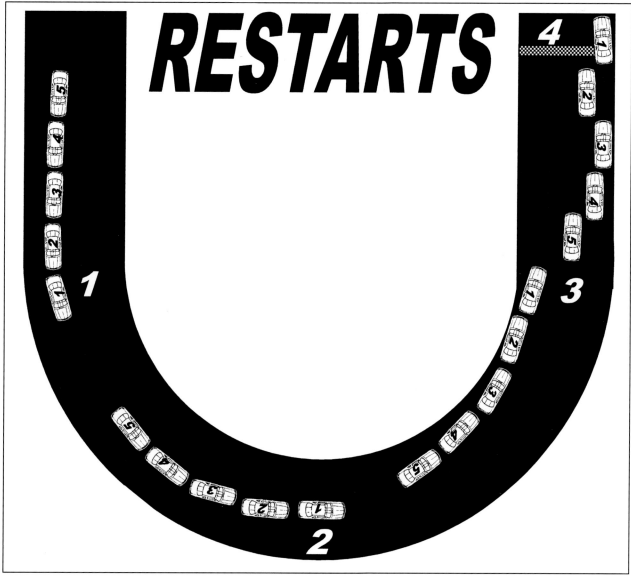

RESTARTS

In this scene, the No. 2 car creates a gap behind the leader at position 3 in order to get a jump on the green flag and a run on the leader. While this works on occasion, it most often backfires on the second place car. But if it's late in the race, and it's the only shot at the lead, go for it!

single file in most cases for short track racing. When double file restarts are used, such as in the major NASCAR divisions, then they are very much like a race start.

If you are in the lead on a single file restart, the most important tactic is to hold a rpm level that is advantageous for you. You should watch the car behind, and accelerate if you see the car behind drop back to get a run on you at the green. You can also try to speed up slightly, then slow gradually so that the following car is out of phase and you are on the throttle when the green flies. If you mistime this, you can be easily passed, so this technique does have its downside.

If you are behind, you have two options. First, the most conservative tactic is to stay right on the bumper of the car ahead and accelerate with that car or when the green comes out. This is a safe restart.

Second, you can trail behind a car length or so, attempting to time your acceleration just before the green comes on. This will give you a jump on the car ahead, unless your action is mistimed, and then you're in trouble. Remember that in nearly all stock car racing associations, you cannot pass, or even pull out of line to pass on a start or restart before crossing the start/finish line. So know your local rules or be ready for the black flag.

Passing Techniques and Defending Position

Passing is a skill that takes time, patience, and precise judgement, and it certainly can be one of the most difficult skills to develop. If one car is much faster than another, a pass can be made with relative ease. If two cars and drivers are evenly matched, it can be a long, difficult process. Like passing, defending position is an art. To properly defend position, a driver must drive quick laps and skillfully place the car on lines in which it is difficult or impossible for the chasing driver to pass.

Lap after lap, the leader is able to hold off the second place car on a half-mile, semibanked short track. After about 20 laps, the following driver gets by the leader under braking going into Turn One. The pass looks easy, but the reality is that the driver making the pass spent those 20 laps setting up the leader for a single shot at the Number One spot. Patience is paramount, but the tactics involved relate to the way tires make traction, and the driver's ability to use those physical characteristics of race tires.

As we've discussed, tires make traction in any direction—braking, accelerating and cornering. You can use all of the traction for cornering or for braking/accelerating; or you can split the traction between the two.

Passing is an art. The track's configuration, a car's handling, and the line a competitior's car is taking dictate where and how the driver can make a pass. Here, Alan Kulwicki makes an inside pass on Richard Petty. *Nigel Kinrade*

Sometimes the fastest line into a corner requires earlier braking, a later turn-in and a more distinct separation of braking and cornering. You can brake later by taking a straighter line and earlier turn-in for the corner, but your speed in mid-turn will be slower. The same applies to the exit of a corner. The straighter your exit line, the harder you can accelerate, because the rear tires will have more traction available for acceleration, less for cornering. This may not always be the fastest way around the whole track, but this technique allows a chasing driver to pass another driver, if the technique is used aggressively and timed perfectly. The illustration shows a braking and an acceleration pass.

SHORT TRACK PASSING

Let's say you've been following the Number 30 car for about 20 laps, looking for a way

Micheal Waltrip leads Harry Gant through a turn at the 1993 Hanes 500. Gant tries to place his car underneath Waltrip, but there isn't enough room because Waltrip is blocking the inside racing line. If Gant can get a better drive out of the corner and get underneath Waltrip, he can execute a text book acceleration pass. *Nigel Kinrade*

around. You have a slight advantage on long runs exiting Turn Four, so you plan to use that advantage to make a pass. Making a pass on a car that is equal to yours is tough. It could take another 10 to 20 laps to actually get around the leading car.

In order to make the pass, you must get a run on the Number 30 exiting Turn Four so that you can get along side under braking going into Turn One. If you can get your front wheel alongside the Number 30 rear wheel, then you can run side by side for a few laps on the preferred inside groove. Eventually, you will be able to gain a clear advantage.

Under braking, your car is no faster than the Number 30. To make a successful run on the straight, you need to change your line slightly in mid-corner. You need to take full advantage of your superior exit speed by getting on the power even earlier and a little harder. To do this, you must have the steering wheel straighter so that the rear tires have more forward bite off the turn. This will allow harder acceleration. If you can get on the throttle sooner, you make the straightaway a little longer, again adding to your advantage. We're not talking car lengths here, maybe a couple of feet at best. But that will be enough to get you alongside going into Turn One.

Exiting Turn Two, you are right on the bumper of the Number 30 car. Heading into Turn Three, you brake a little earlier and turn in sooner than normal. This allows you to rotate your car sooner at the apex between turns Three and Four. By doing this, you can unwind the steering wheel sooner and exit Four in a straighter line than normal. This is not the fastest way around the track, but it is the fastest way down the front straight. Going in you lose a half a car length, but your speed reduction and altered line allow you to accelerate sooner. You gain back that half-length well before the starter's stand and you have momentum working for you. Without giving up that half a car length going in, you would not be able to have a speed advantage on the straight. We are only looking at a 1- to 2-mile-per-hour advantage.

At the starter's stand, you pull to the left and use your momentum to get your front bumper even with the Number 30's rear bumper. Unless you can extend your advantage under braking, you will need to back off going into Turn One, losing the advantage. It may take several attempts to make the pass.

To get an advantage under braking, you will need to drive into the corner straighter than normal so that more of the tire's traction can be used for braking. If you can wait until the Number 30 car's driver gets on the binders to apply your brakes, then you can get alongside, at least so that your front wheel is alongside his rear wheel. The Number 30 car must leave you room at that point or risk a spin if he drives his inside rear quarter into your right front fender. You will gain another foot or two through the mid-part of the turn, so that your front bumper is now at the Number 30's A-pillar.

It will likely take another 5 to 10 laps to get clear ahead of the Number 30. At this point, you must use the track to your advantage. Being on the inside, you can choose the fastest line, as long as you leave the Number 30 car racing room to the outside. Going into the turns, you want to take the ideal line into the turn under braking. This is the line that allows you to position the car for optimum acceleration just past mid-turn. The other driver will gain a slight advantage going in and through the middle of the turn. It will be tempting to turn in early so that you have more racing room, but that will give the Number 30 car an advantage and he will get the lead back.

The same applies to the exit. You must drive the Number 30 car right up to the wall, leaving him just enough room to stay off the fence and off your right side. The outside car has a slight advantage exiting the turns. If you leave more room than the absolute minimum, that advantage gets bigger, and you will lose your hard-earned position. But if your nerves are made of steel, you maintain the highest levels of concentration and make no significant mistakes, you will eventually pull clear of the Number 30 car.

PLANNING PASSES

Ten laps into the feature, you're hounding the leader. You attempt a pass under braking to the inside, but the other car is a little too quick. At the next turn, you try again, getting your nose under the other car's rear quarter panel. But your car starts to push and you have to back off. You know you're a little quicker, but you just can't get by. You keep right on the leader's decklid, but he keeps holding you off. If you try to pass under braking, the car pushes, and you can't seem to get a good run off the corners to pass on the straight. With five laps left in the race, the leader pulls away slightly.

You finish second, feeling frustrated, since you know that you had a faster car.

This is a common scenario in all forms of racing. First, let's look at the reality of making passes. Sometimes the other driver is very good at defending his or her position. You may never be able to get by. On the other hand, with a good game plan, you can increase your odds at making a pass that will stick.

Lateral track position is very important for making passes, and is often overlooked by drivers. In view 1, The No. 2 car is taking an earlier turn-in line to pass low under braking. The lateral position of No. 1 allows this to happen. In view 2, the No. 1 car defends low with an early turn-in, leaving the door open to the outside. The No. 2 can set up for an acceleration pass at the exit, with a little patience and flawless execution. In view 3, the No. 2 car can do nothing but follow the leader, since the defensive line of No. 1 was perfectly executed. Save the attempt for another turn. In view 4, the driver of No. 1 has taken a defensive line going in, allowing No. 2 to overlap high. But No. 1 has altered his line to hold the No. 2 car high. The No. 2 cannot turn down to the apex until the No. 1 turns in. If No. 1 holds No. 2 high through the midsection of the turn, No. 2 will be forced to drop in behind No. 1.

MAKING PASSES

There are four ways to pass another car. The easiest is when the other driver makes a mistake. However, you must be in position to take advantage of that mistake when it happens. If you're not ready, you will miss the opportunity. The closer you are to the front, the fewer opportunities will be presented.

> Down the straightaway is the best place to pass, but that usually means you have carry more momentum off the corner than the car ahead of you to make the pass.
>
> *–Jeff Gordon*

> Normally, the best place to pass on a short track is coming off the corners. If you can get up underneath somebody coming off the corner and out-accelerate them, that's the best place.
>
> *–Terry Labonte*

> To draft by a car, you back away from the car in front of you to get momentum and know when you pull out that you can completely make the pass.
>
> *–Jeff Gordon*

> To set up another car for a pass, you figure out where you're strong and where they're weak, and try to take advantage of their weak spot.
>
> *–Jeff Burton*

The most common pass is under braking entering a corner. This pass requires good judgment and a solid plan, and it can take several laps to set up. Mid-corner passes are often easy if the other car has a small handling problem. Mid-corner passes are very difficult if the cars are equal, unless the lead car makes a mistake. The mid-corner pass is most often used when the track has two (or more) grooves. The corner exit pass is the safest, and this can be accomplished by getting on the power sooner and carrying momentum down the straightaway. This often looks like a drafting pass (and sometimes is on a superspeedway or road course), or by late braking. In reality, this pass is made with corner exit speed, even if

the pass is not completed until the entry to the next corner under braking.

PASSING SCENARIOS

In the following scenarios, two cars are used to illustrate common passing situations. The Number 2 car is the car making the passes, and the Number 7 car is the leading car being passed.

Scenario 1
Corner Entry Pass Under Braking

In this situation, the driver of the Number 2 car brakes later than Number 7. He can do this by turning into the corner sooner and taking a straighter line into the corner. Since Number 2 is using less traction for turning (straighter line), more traction is available for braking. The driver of Number 2 is able to make the pass, but will be slower at mid turn and must then defend position exiting the cor-

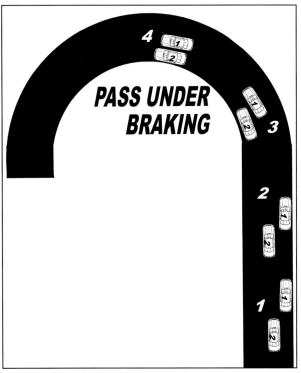

The easiest pass to make is under braking. To do this, you need to get a strong exit from the previous turn, so that you get a run (1) on the car ahead. Without the run, it will be very difficult to make the pass cleanly. At the braking point (2), you will pull to the inside and take slightly straighter line into the corner so that you can brake a little later. If the car ahead turns in early, this will not work. At 3, you should position your car below the car you are trying pass. Hold your line low and keep the other car high, so that he cannot get a run on you at the exit (4).

ner. The driver of Number 2 is vulnerable to being passed again on the straight.

Scenario 2
Corner Exit Pass Under Acceleration

Here the driver of Number 2 takes a higher line in mid-turn, sacrificing speed to take a straight line on the exit. The driver of Number 7 takes the overall fastest line. Number 2 can get on the power sooner and harder with the late apex exit line. If Number 2 has not lost ground to Number 7 going into the corner, the straighter line out of the corner will let him carry more speed down the straight. This will allow Number 2 to gain position on the inside of the straight and under braking.

ALTERNATE LINES

Unless the other driver makes a mistake, the driver will hold the preferred line into, through, and out of the corners. That means to make a pass, you must drive off the best path through the corner, or at least through some portion of the corner. This is precisely why passing an equal car is so difficult.

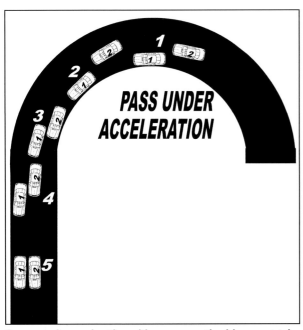

To pass under acceleration exiting a corner, the driver must take a later apex line going in to (1). As the driver begins to accelerate, he or she should stay high and leave a small gap to the car ahead (2). By Turn 3, the car is straighter and able to accelerate a little sooner and harder than the other car, so you will carry more speed out of the turn. The driver now has position and momentum (4) and should begin to pull ahead before entering the next turn (5).

The key to making a pass is to choose an alternate path that allows you to accomplish your goal. Here are two examples. If your goal is to pass under braking, how can you improve braking performance? On most short tracks, you brake and turn (at least a little) at the same time. Part of the tire's

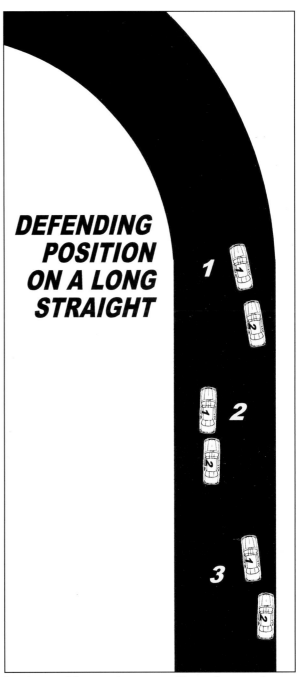

On a long straightaway where an attacking car is attempting to draft by, move to the inside to break the draft and make the attacker go to the outside for a pass attempt. Move back high as the next corner approaches to get the optimum line through the corner.

traction is used for cornering, the rest for braking. You must change the percentage if you want to outbrake your rival. Take a straighter line into the corner so more of the tire traction can be used for braking. There will be a price to pay in mid-corner, however. Since you entered straighter, you must now rotate the car more for the exit. You will have to sacrifice mid-corner speed to pass under braking, but you must be in a position to get on the power early, or the car you pass entering the turn will pull ahead of you at the exit.

In this scenario, you can get underneath the lead car going into the turn, and that driver cannot rotate until you rotate. The trick is to rotate your car at the best time for you, forcing the other driver to rotate after you do. Then you can drive off the corner on the line that allows you the best corner exit acceleration.

The same applies to passing at the exit. Drive a different line into and through the turn that allows you to use more tire traction for acceleration earlier

> **If you want a guy to pass you, you'll point to which side. If something happens in front of you, you put your arm up and wave to let them know that something is going on.**
>
> *–Jeff Burton*

than the other car. This allows you to carry more momentum down the straight, giving you the advantage into the next turn. Many drivers make a crucial mistake when doing this, which negates the effort. If you follow the lead car too closely into and through the turn, any momentum advantage you gain will be lost, because you will have to slow to keep from hitting the car ahead. A clear mental picture of your desired path through the turn, and well-executed timing will allow you to make the pass more easily, and to stay ahead.

TRACK POSITION

Lateral track position is one of the keys to passing. This is where you are left to right, relative to the car you are trying to pass. When alongside another car, it is common courtesy and good track etiquette to leave the other car racing room. Two questions arise here. How much room do you leave and when must you leave room? If you are on the inside, you

> **Usually when you're leading the race, your car is really working good. A lot of times, you're running easier leading the race than when you're running third trying to keep up.**
>
> *–Terry Labonte*

should leave just over a car width to the outside wall. How much over a car width? How good is your judgment, or how large is your pit crew? A foot should be considered liberal. The same applies to leaving room for a car trying to pass to the inside.

> **With 10 laps to go, the ideal position to be in is leading.**
>
> *–Terry Labonte*

> **You look in the mirror constantly with your peripheral vision. It may be 10 times a lap. It depends.**
>
> *–Terry Labonte*

The second question is more of a judgment call. When do you need to leave racing room for the other car? Another rule of thumb applies here. You should leave room when the other car is within your peripheral vision, or when your spotter tells you that the other car has moved along side you. If you try to pass to the inside going into a corner, expect the other driver to close the door if he cannot see you alongside. I always assume the other driver cannot see me unless my nose is at least even with his B-pillar. And don't always rely on the spotter to give accurate information, especially at a short track where visibility is often obstructed. On the other hand, if you do not see the car trying to get underneath you, or you attempt to slam the door shut from the outside, who is really at risk? The car lower and slightly behind usually is at less risk. If you are higher and ahead and you turn down, your rear quarter panel will likely hit the front of the lower car. Giving way is usually better than a spin or a trip into the fence. Great care must be taken in this situation. You really need to decide in advance how far you are willing to push either situation before it arises, and be willing to accept the consequences of your decision regardless of the outcome. If you do not accept the consequences, the time you spend fuming over the situation will render you ineffective as a driver. Most often the lower car continues to race, and the lead car spins. It is really important to know where you want to be on the race track, and to know where the other cars are.

PASSING AND TIRES

In the earlier scenario, one of the factors keeping the second-place driver behind was the state of the tires on that car. When you attempt a mad dog pass under braking, the front tires heat up. That means less traction, so the pass becomes less likely to succeed. Do this for three or four corners in a row, and the tires get even hotter. The car starts to push, and as the race progresses, the situation gets

> You look at what the other cars are doing, how they're handling, and try to take advantage of their weaknesses.
>
> –Jeff Burton

worse. To make a successful pass requires tires that are at their optimum for the job. You need to keep the tires cool while waiting for an opportunity. At this stage, it is best to set up for the fastest possible run off one corner. This requires cooling rear tires for peak traction and using the front tires for out-braking into the next turn when they are at their optimum traction. This makes the pass more certain and more likely to stick.

> A lot of times, if you don't use patience when attempting a pass, you won't finish the race. But sometimes, you don't have to be patient. A restart with 10 laps to go, you don't have time for patience.
>
> –Ricky Rudd

If you abuse your tires, you lose traction and control. Passes become more and more difficult. You soon find yourself in a defensive position, trying to hold off the cars behind you. If you abuse your tires early in the race, you will be a sitting duck at the end of the race or long green run. It is also helpful to create a car setup that allows for easier passing. And if you know you will need to run off-line to make passes, you need to get the car working for off-line situations, then practice driving on the most likely passing lines. This will give you a distinct advantage.

PATIENCE

It has been said often that patience is a virtue. Those words were meant for the race driver in a passing situation. Patience is a critical factor in several ways. A patient driver attempting to make a pass has several advantages. He or she is more open to developing situations. Typically, the driver is in a better position to take advantage of mistakes by others and is more likely to force mistakes by other drivers. The driver crashes less, is more prone to focus attention on most important priorities, and manages tires more effectively. In wheel-to-wheel racing, he or she is rarely passed again and is often more effective at holding off pass attempts.

> You can intimidate the driver behind you by staying in front of him. If you stay in front long enough that usually wears him down and frustrates him enough to be able to intimidate him. Intimidation, however, comes easier if you're behind than if you're in front.
>
> –Jeff Gordon

The impatient driver most often uses up the tires quickly, misses opportunities, gets passed easily, suffers from red mist (clouded judgment), often hits the lead car while trying to pass, fades as the race progresses, and rarely wins.

Patience, like most virtues, requires commitment and practice. The effort is worthwhile.

> I know the personalities of the other drivers. I know who will give me a certain amount of room and who won't, and I base my strategy for passing them on that.
>
> –Terry Labonte

THE PSYCHOLOGY OF PASSING

The psychological side of passing works like most areas of racing: confidence works wonders. If you believe you can make a pass, you have a much better chance. If you're not sure, the odds work against you.

The other side of the equation is the psych job. Some drivers watch their mirrors too closely and are affected by pressure; others are not. One of the most common tools that can be used effectively is to apply constant pressure to the lead driver. This can be done with consistent pass attempts, either in the same place or in varying locations. The danger here is that by attacking, you can overheat tires, making yourself vulnerable to passing attacks. Possibly the best way to intimidate is to apply pressure through consistent driving, always being in the exact same place on the track, lap after lap.

> **You can aggravate the driver ahead by driving up under his fuel cell as far as you can. It lightens the back tires up, and it gets to be a handful after a period of time.**
>
> *–Ricky Rudd*

The most effective method of psyching is to make a clean pass quickly and easily while at the same time making it very difficult for others to pass you. By doing that, it becomes easier to make passes on all drivers later. That is how Dale Earnhardt became the "Intimidator." Again, confidence in your ability and commitment to making the move are your greatest assets.

PASSING STRATEGIES

A strategy is a predetermined plan. Relative to passing other cars, creating a plan in advance is important for success. The plan is not something like "I'll pass car Number 5 on the 10th lap." It is a plan to act in situations and respond to circumstances. The elements of your plan should include:

- **Where you can best make a pass**
- **Whether the best time to attack is early or late in the race**
- **How a specific driver may respond to pressure.**
- **Whether a specific driver is prone to making mistakes or overdriving the tires**
- **How to set up your car for the race**

LAPPING TRAFFIC

One of the most important skills a driver can develop is the ability to lap slower traffic without losing time or taking unnecessary risks. Judgment and timing are the keys to lapping traffic, or being lapped. The single most important quality is managing your field of vision. The drivers who are best at negotiating traffic look ahead so that anticipation time is lengthened. A visual field that is too short will limit anticipation, and make passing much more difficult.

> **The best place to pass on a superspeedway depends on the race track and tends to move around. At Daytona, we have three lanes wide of racing, so it depends on who's lined up in which lane and who you want to line up with. You'll see the banking start to flatten out and transition onto the straightaway, and that's about the time you start to unwind the steering wheel.**
>
> *–Ricky Rudd*

> **There's not a good place to pace on a superspeedway. It's all about momentum. Wherever you gain that momentum is where you'll try to pass. Sometimes the outside is blocked, so you go to the inside. If the inside is blocked, you do it to the outside.**
>
> *–Ricky Rudd*

Drivers skilled in lapping traffic also see situations develop in advance. Visual fields influence this skill, but so does the ability to see holes opening. This requires an open mind and the ability to not be judgmental of developing situations. The situation is neither good nor bad. By seeing the reality of the situation, and being able to respond to it

> **To pass someone, they're running your line, so you pretty much have to get out of your normal line to outmaneuver them.**
>
> *–Ricky Rudd*

quickly, you have the best chance of taking advantage of developments as they occur. It is important to remember that the entire racing surface is fair game. It also pays to know the rules thoroughly.

Winning races is the essence of racing. It is rare to win a race without having to pass other cars. Developing passing skills is one of the most important areas a driver can work on to increase the odds of winning races.

DEFENDING POSITION

For the last 10 laps, the Number 9 car has been hounding you, right on your rear bumper. While he has moved to the inside to take a look, he has yet to make a serious attempt to pass you, but you know it's coming. Going into Turn One, the Number 9 car pulls inside under braking, just getting alongside by a few inches, but your better line allows you to stay ahead by mid-turn.

You know he will try the same move going into Turn Three, so you turn in earlier than normal to fend him off. He stays higher than normal, attempting to get a run on you off of Turn Four. You look for him in your mirror along the straight and he's gaining ground. You plan to turn in early again to hold off his charge, checking your mirror at the end of the straight. You look in the mirror at the wrong time and the instantaneous distraction causes you to miss your turn-in and braking point for the early turn-in line you wanted to use to defend your position. Now you cannot place the car exactly where you wanted, even though you are on what would normally be a fast line. You haven't overdriven the car or track, but you are not in the best possible position to hold off the Number 9 car. He goes low, putting his front bumper even with your B-pillar. You run side-by-side for the last 10 laps of the race, but he has the advantage coming out of the turns and nips you at the finish by 5 feet. It's an exciting finish to a very tough race, but you're disappointed at letting a victory slip away in the last few laps.

This scenario is common. No driving mistakes were made in this scene, but a misuse of attention at a crucial moment allowed the Number 9 car to find a hole just big enough to allow an advantage and snatch a victory. In this case, paying attention to the most important elements *at the right time* is critical. Looking in the mirror on the straight was a good use of attention at a good time. The glance into the mirror at the end of the straight was just enough of a

> **You can change your line to defend position, especially late in the race. You do whatever you have to do.**
>
> *–Jeff Burton*

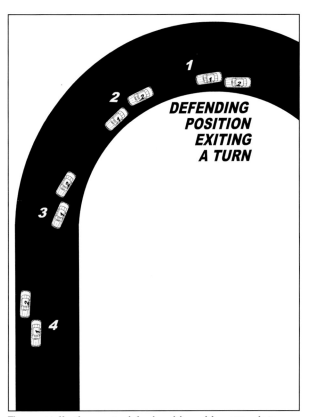

The most effective way to defend position exiting a turn is to leave no room for the attacking car in mid-turn (1), then take a late exit line (2,3,4), so that you get the best acceleration out of the corner and down the following straight.

> **When coming up on a lapped car, you'll anticipate what they're doing by about two laps before you'll try to pass. With the help of a spotter, you may see that they are running low about 90 percent of the time, so you take that into consideration and not get yourself in a position where you're boxed in on the low side of the race track by slower cars. You start working your groove up to the outside before you get there.**
>
> *–Ricky Rudd*

distraction to cause the driver to miss the spot where he wanted to turn in, even though his line was good and he was right on the limits of traction without overdriving. Missing that mark by only 3 or 4 feet was enough to create an opportunity for the driver of the Number 9 to gain an important, and race-winning position. At that critical moment, looking in the mirror took crucial attention away from driving the perfect line to defend position, even though the driver knew that that line was the best way to defend position. The small glitch in attention was all that was needed to lose position. There are three keys to defending position.

Drive Perfect Laps at the Limit

The best way to defend position is to be decisively faster than the following car or cars. Remember these points:

- **Focus attention on your own driving**
- **Know who's behind you, but drive your race**
- **Minimize steering inputs**
- **Manage your tires so you stay fast**

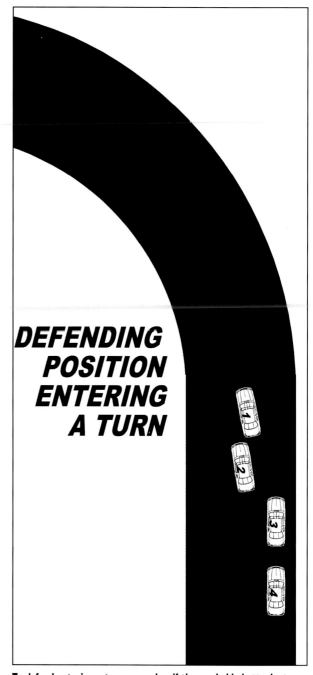

DEFENDING POSITION ENTERING A TURN

To defend entering a turn, move low if the car behind attacks to the inside. Spotter input is helpful here, because looking in the mirror too long or too often is distracting and can cause you to miss a reference point or overdrive the entry of the corner.

Alter Your Line

If the following car is attacking, alter your line to make it as difficult as possible for the other car. Lap times no longer matter. Here are some pointers:

- **Generally defend the inside of the track**
- **Take an early turn-in line going into the turns**

- Force the other car to attempt an outside pass under braking
- Take an exit line that allows you to accelerate as early as possible
- On a long straight, try to break the draft on the following car
- If the following car attempts to pass on the outside under braking, move up the track in mid-turn to force the other car higher

Focus on the Right Priorities

It is always best to drive your own race. You need to be aware of the position of following cars by using your mirror and your spotter, but do it when you can afford to spend the attention such as on the straights. If you focus on going fast, it makes the other driver's job of getting around you more difficult. If you must defend position from an attack,

> I want to be in the lead with one lap to go.
>
> *–Jeff Burton*

focus on driving a defensive line, not on what the other driver is doing. If you spend attention on his car, your performance will suffer and his job becomes much easier.

You need to have a strategy to defend position. Study the scenarios in the chapter on passing, but from a defensive position. Here are some tips: Manage your tires according to a pre-race plan; know what the drivers who may be attacking are likely to do; decide ahead how you will defend if you come under attack; stick to your game plan.

Sometimes the attacking car is just plain faster. Attempting to defend against a faster car can often cause you to overdrive, overheat the tires and lose more positions. When this is the case, make it easy for the other driver to get by. It will save you time and make it less likely for other cars to get close enough to attack. Other times, the attacking driver is overdriving the car to get around you. He will likely burn down his tires within a few laps, so be *patient*! When his tires go off, you will get back by easily.

FOURTEEN

How the Driver Affects Handling

A novice driver has to contend with a new car, track, team, and many other elements. At a time when a driver is trying to build basic driving skills, it can be difficult to distinguish the difference between a driving problem and a setup problem. Many team sand drivers have unwittingly changed a car's setup in an attempt to resolve an unrecognized driver problem.

During hot laps, a driver picks up a considerable push in mid-turn after about three quick laps. He comes into the pits for an adjustment. The crew adds a little stagger and he goes back out. On his first lap at speed, the car gets real loose going into Turn One. He nearly spins, but he manages to get the car gathered up. He goes back into the pits for another change, this time stiffening the front anti-roll bar. The loose condition disappears going in on cool tires, but the push is worse than ever in mid-turn after tires arrive at operating temperature. He comes back in, confused about what to do next.

This driver probably did not consider all of the options available when the mid-turn push was first encountered. One of the most likely causes is the driver. Driver error should always be considered when handling problems crop up. There are several items to consider when analyzing handling problems. The first is to confirm or eliminate the driver as a possible cause. Keep in mind, the driver influences weight transfer and tire traction at each corner of the car in a variety of situations. If the driver is too hard on the

Although this accident resulted from contact with another car, student racers should study it closely because this can be the result if overdriving occurs. *Paul Johnson/Speed Sports Photography*

throttle, he can cause either a push or a loose condition, depending on what he does with the throttle pedal. How and when the driver uses any of the controls will often cause or cure a perceived handling problem.

DRIVER-INDUCED HANDLING PROBLEMS

The opening scenario is common. But how does it happen? It's incredibly easy for a driver to cause this problem. If the driver comes into the corner too hot under hard braking, and attempts to rotate the car while applying too much brake pedal pressure, then a significant push is created. Ironically, it can also cause the car to get loose. If the car has too much brake bias to the rear, a loose car can result under heavy braking while steering; too much front bias and the situation reverses. A slight roll couple bias can have the same effect. Too much front roll couple causes a push, too much rear will create a loose situation.

> **A driver in some situations can induce handling problems by the way he drives a corner. But modern drivers are pretty aware of changing the entry lines into a corner. That's way you see some guys running low and some run high because maybe they're not running good down low even though they know they need to be down low. They're faster under the circumstances on the top of the race track. A few years ago some of the drivers didn't have the feel that drivers have today, so they could have caused handling problems.**
>
> *–Ricky Rudd*

The overriding factor here is the driver. If the driver brakes too hard and tries to rotate the car (more steering wheel lock applied by the driver while braking), the car will have a handling problem just like the one described in the opening scene. The situation may not appear again until the tires get hot. This will typically cause the car to push since the front tires may be overheating due to heavy braking going into the corners. The situation will only get worse as the tires get hotter and begin to wear.

> **Understanding race car dynamics is a very important point. It's very important to know your car, know the setup underneath the car. It allows you to communicate better with the crew chief and your team to set up the car.**
>
> *–Jeff Gordon*

Even if a car is perfectly neutral, the driver can cause a handling problem by making the steering motion too quickly or abruptly. Jerking the steering wheel can cause the front tire slip angles to increase suddenly relative to the rear tire slip angles, causing a push to begin, which can linger even though the rear tire slip angles eventually catch up to the front slip angles.

Corner exit handling problems can also be driver-caused. The most common situation is wheel spin exiting a turn. The driver applying the throttle pedal too quickly causes the wheel spin condition. More crossweight may reduce this, but the driver has considerable influence over the situation. Just like the entry of a turn, the same action by the driver could cause the exact opposite problem. A push at the exit of the turn can also be driver induced, simply by accelerating too hard with too much steering lock. If the relative amount of drive torque available is too little to cause wheel spin, the weight transfer due to acceleration can increase rear tire traction while reducing front tire traction. This change in balance often causes a push at the exit of a turn when wheel spin is not likely to occur. In each case, the driver is misusing the controls, which upsets the handling balance.

INCORRECTLY FIXING DRIVING PROBLEMS WITH SETUP CHANGES

The temptation for a driver is always to "fix" the problem by changing the setup of the car. Drivers, or crew chiefs for that matter, rarely look to the driver as the cause of a handling problem. More often than not, the driver is the cause of these types of handling problems, especially if the driver is inexperienced, new to a given car or class, or new to a given race track. It is also likely if the driver is not sensitive to changing traction as the track conditions change or tire grip diminishes.

Jeff Gordon has established himself as a top driver in the Winston Cup championship because he is able to consistently get the most from his car. A novice driver must accurately communicate the behavior of the car to his crew chief or mechanic. With time, the team should be able to find the best setup and make adjustments to match changing track conditions during a race. *Paul Johnson/Speed Sports Photography*

Attempting to change the setup to cure driver-induced handling ills will likely cause more handling ills and hurt overall car performance. For example, if the car is loose at the exit because of wheel spin, more crossweight may help. But that may cause a push going into the turns. And even if the increased crossweight reduces or eliminates the wheel spin, the car may now push at the exit also. The example in the opening scenario indicates what could happen at the turn entry. There are many other possibilities! Any time a car is adjusted to fix a driver-caused handling problem, some other problem will occur, usually creating a more serious situation. To achieve the best possible, fastest setup, driver errors need to be minimized, especially during transitional periods such as entering and exiting corners. If the driver continues to upset the delicate balance of the car during these crucial phases of transition, handling problems will persist.

ELIMINATING DRIVER-INDUCED HANDLING PROBLEMS

The first step in curing driver-induced handling ills is to recognize that the driver may be the cause of the problem. This can be very difficult for two reasons. First, handling problems can be easily masked since several different scenarios can be the cause for a given problem. Second, it can be difficult for drivers to have the insight and honesty needed to look within for the problem. It takes courage and commitment to confront yourself and your ego to seek the truth. Several clues help determine whether the car or the driver is the root of the problem. If the problem is inconsistent, it is most likely driver induced.

If a problem occurs at every similar type of turn, it is most likely, but not always, setup related. On road courses, if a problem occurs on either left or right turns only, it is likely setup related. If the problem occurs at one turn only or one segment of a turn, it is likely driver induced.

IMPROVING YOUR DRIVING TECHNIQUE

Driver control errors cause handling problems, and the errors fall into two categories, all occurring during transitions. Abrupt control responses, jerking the steering wheel, hitting the brake pedal too hard, or nailing the throttle to the floor, are the usual problems. Second, the timing of control use may be off. Turning the steering wheel too soon or too late going into a turn can upset the car, causing problems. The same applies to the brake and throttle pedals. Smooth movements of the controls timed perfectly will eliminate most of the driver-induced handling problems.

Here are some examples. Turning the steering wheel too quickly at the entry to a turn can cause a push or loose condition, as previously described. This relates closely to the use of the brakes in unison with steering. If the steering wheel is turned too quickly while the brakes are applied too much going into a turn, the tires will be overloaded. The tires can steer and decelerate the car at the same time, but only up to point. The combination of brake and steering cannot exceed the limits of total tire traction. The tires create only so much traction regardless of direction (accelerate or brake, plus turn). The combination can go right to the traction limit, but not exceed it. All of the traction can be used to turn, or to brake, or some combination of the two. If the limit is exceeded, the tires will slide, usually at one end of the car before the other. If the front tires lose traction first, a push or understeer condition is the result.

The driver is in complete control of this. More steering means less brake; more brake means less steering. If you need to turn the wheel while braking at the limits of tire traction, the tires cannot do the job. Steering requires less traction to be used for braking. The more steering required, the less braking you can use. If all the traction is needed for turning, then no braking can be used, and vice versa.

The same situation applies to the corner exit. More traction for acceleration requires less steering lock by the driver. Maximum traction efficiency requires you to stay on the limit of the traction circle. If you go over the limit of the traction circle by asking the tires to do more work than they can, a handling problem will occur.

Think of the throttle and brake pedals as being attached to the steering wheel. More pressure on the pedal means less steering lock. More steering lock means less pressure on the pedals. Too much steering or too much pedal pressure causes tire traction limits to be exceeded.

As you enter a turn under braking, you must ease off the brake pedal in order to stay within the limits of traction. At some point in the turn, all of the traction must be used for cornering, so the brakes are released and the car balanced with the throttle (without acceleration). At the exit of a turn, to facilitate acceleration down the straights, the steering wheel must be unwound. If it is not, a handling problem, caused by the driver, will occur. The big question is finding the balance between pedal application and steering wheel lock angle. It's like walking a tightrope. Too much of either will cause the fine balance to be lost and the car will fall off the desired path. Too little will be slow. The key to being a fast race driver is learning to keep the car balanced on the edge of traction.

Finally, timing in the use of control is crucial for fast driving. Turning in too early can require using more steering lock midway into a turn. This should require a reduction in braking force, but then you may enter the corner with too much speed. This circumstance may also alter your line around the corner. Braking too late or turning in too late, not rotating the car at the best place on the track, can force you to slow the car to avert disaster. Timing can be thrown off if control movements are too slow. The combination of smooth control use (perfect balance between pedal and steering inputs) and precise timing make driving a race car an art form. Being off by five degrees of steering wheel angle, 10 pounds on brake pedal pressure, or a tenth of a second on timing can cost valuable hundredths of a second on the race track. True speed is found by perfecting your skills in these areas.

THE OVERALL GOAL

It is important to keep in mind that the singular goal is to get around the race track as fast as possible, whether for a single lap or an entire race. Race car dynamics relate ultimately to tire traction at the tire contact patch. Optimizing traction on the complete car means faster lap times. We can do this by manipulating the chassis components and the driver's steering, braking, and accelerator inputs. Not only does the driver operate the controls, but the driver's input concerning what the car is doing at specific points on the race track plays a paramount role in success. The team doing the best job of this—optimizing traction on the complete car—will be in the top five. From there, tactics, strategy, execution, and maybe a little luck will determine the winner.

Tire Management and Traction

A ll professional race drivers realize the importance of tire management and utilizing maximum available traction. A smooth, seasoned driver will economically manage tires until a pivotal portion of the race. At that time, the veteran driver will run at 100 percent and extract all available tire performance if necessary. Most drivers try to win the race at the slowest possible speed. On the other side of a spectrum, many novice drivers fall into the trap of overdriving the car at the wrong stage of the race, overheating the tires, and losing position.

After the feature race, a driver tells his crew chief, "With about 20 laps left, my tires started to go away. My car got real loose comin' off the turns and I just couldn't keep up the pace." How many times have you heard comments like these in a post-race interview? You may have even made comments like this yourself. Tires "going off" are a common problem in racing. The real question is the cause. Often times, a driver blames Goodyear or Hoosier. In the majority of cases, the real culprit is the driver or, sometimes, the car setup, or a combination of the two. Because the driver literally controls heat buildup in the tires, the driver can control and modulate tire wear. Even gaining one total lap of improved performance can offer an important advantage in any race. There are several ways the driver can manage tires to gain an advantage.

Mark Martin and other top drivers manage their tires because a race can be won or lost depending on tire health. If a driver drives too hard and wears out the tires before a scheduled pit stop or at a critical part of the race, he or she will lose track position. *Nigel Kinrade*

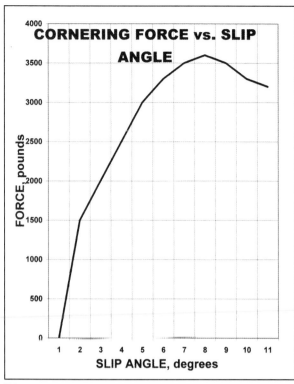

CORNERING FORCE vs. SLIP ANGLE

This graph shows cornering force versus tire slip angle. At 6.5 degrees of slip angle, the cornering force is the same as 7.5 degrees of slip angle. The driver at 6.5 degrees slip angle isn't any faster than the driver at 7.5 degrees for one lap, but after several laps, the driver at 7.5 degrees slip angle will have hotter tires that are more worn. As a consequence, this will slow the car in the turns and hurt lap times. Turning the steering more slowly and smoothly will allow the driver to drive the car at the lower slip angle.

TIRE TERMINOLOGY

Most of you are familiar with the tire terms used here. To ensure we are talking about the same thing, several important terms will be discussed.

Slip Angle—The slip angle of a tire refers to the difference in direction of the tire tread and the wheel. The wheel will turn farther than the tire tread on the ground. The angle between these is the slip angle. The tire creates maximum traction at some slip angle. A smaller- or larger-than-optimum slip angle means less traction. Stiff sidewalls operate in a lower range of slip angles than more flexible sidewall tires. The best drivers will operate at the lowest possible slip angle within the range of maximum traction. If a car pushes, the front tires have a greater slip angle than the rear, and the driver will turn the steering wheel more than if the handling is neutral. The opposite is true for a loose condition.

> Tire scrub on a speedway reduces speed, so the guys do a lot of work on the car to reduce that.
>
> *—Terry Labonte*

Tire Scrub—Anytime the steering wheel is turned, the tires scrub against the track surface. The more the steering is turned, the greater the tire scrub becomes. More scrub means more friction and less speed. Tire scrub also heats the tires more. Turning the steering wheel is like applying the brakes. It slows the car and heats the tires.

Tire Contact Patch—The portion of the tire actually on the racing surface.

Lateral Acceleration—This is cornering force. Any time a car changes direction, an acceleration is created. The lateral acceleration will increase as cornering speed goes up or turn radius decreases. The force is proportional to the acceleration.

Wheel Lock-Up—This occurs when the tire is no longer rolling. A tire cannot steer unless it is rolling.

Nearly every cause of overheated tires can be attributed to the driver. The driver must walk the tightrope between maximum speed and saving the tires for the end of the race or extending life between pit stops. What the driver does with the controls can make a big difference to tire heating and wear. A simple example may help to illustrate the point. During a two-lap qualifying run, the situation is reversed. Tire wear is not a factor, and overheating the tires is rarely a problem. In fact, too little heat is a much greater problem. Getting heat into the tires is a high priority for a qualifying run, especially on the warm-up lap. In this situation, a driver may want to brake especially hard into Turns One and Three and induce a little wheelspin entering the track. But if a driver does this in a race, the tire will "go off" more quickly than necessary. The race itself requires a different plan.

PATIENCE AND DISCIPLINE

During a race, a driver must follow a predetermined plan, one that allows for changing conditions and situations. It is important that a driver show patience so that the tires are not abused, especially during the early part of the race. It is much more desirable to conserve tires early on to gain an

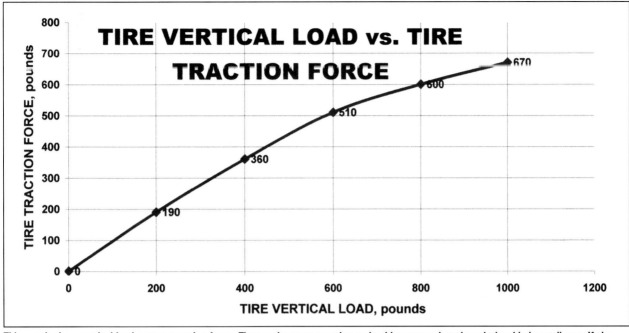

This graph show vertical load versus traction force. Tires make more traction as load increases, but the relationship is not linear. If the load is doubled, the traction force is less than doubled. For this reason, reducing weight transfer is desirable. In addition, the driver needs to use the controls smoothly so that weight transfer is not abrupt.

> **You have to be careful how hard you abuse the tires with the front end settings and things of that nature.**
>
> *–Ricky Rudd*

advantage later. This approach requires considerable discipline (one of the most important attributes of the winning race driver).

Regardless of the urge to push and attack early, it is important to be disciplined and take advantage of situations and mistakes. The most important time to lead is on the last lap. Leading early may make it impossible to run up front at the end. Many factors must be considered in creating a game plan, but when it comes to tire management, discipline and patience can pay big dividends toward the end of the race.

TIRE MANAGEMENT TIPS

Here are some tips that can help you save your tires. Coupled with patience and discipline, you can gain a considerable tire advantage on the race track.

Unwind the steering wheel. More steering lock creates greater tire slip angles and tire scrub: this slows the car and adds heat to the tires. Try to use the minimum turn of the steering wheel to negotiate a corner. And in the turns, try reducing steering lock for brief periods, then add lock as needed. Speed will increase but scrub and tire heat will be reduced the more you do this. You need to remember heavy braking adds heat to the front tires. If you need more heat in the front tires, hard braking will do this. The driver needs to go easy on the brakes to cool the front tires. If the car starts to push, ease off on the brakes for a few laps to cool the front tires. It is important to accelerate hard to heat the rear tires. Some wheel-spin can add heat to the rear tires if needed.

> **Generally, with a full fuel load, you've got new tires. That's usually the best the car is going to be. As the fuel burns off, the tires are going away. We would never run a full fuel load on old tires because it puts a lot of rear weight in the car and abuses the tires, and the car gets extremely loose on you.**
>
> *–Ricky Rudd*

> **Try to keep the tires cleaned off before a restart by weaving back and forth. Drop into a low gear, accelerate two or three times, use the brakes to try to get some heat into the tires.**
>
> *–Ricky Rudd*

Go easy on the throttle to keep the rear tires cool. If the car gets loose, apply the throttle easier at the corner exit. A driver should always be especially careful accelerating off a corner where wheel-spin is possible. Apply the throttle as if an egg were placed between the pedal and your foot; mash hard on the pedal and the egg breaks. Your tires are just as fragile as the egg, so use this kind of discipline to get the best from your tires. You should always keep in mind that wheel-spin kills acceleration. Again, go easy on the throttle, not just to cool the tires, but to manage them at all times. At high speeds, wheel-spin is less likely so the throttle application can be made more quickly. Braking gently saves the tires and the brakes. Most drivers actually turn faster laps during an exercise when they are forced to not use the brakes at all.

Overdriving (braking too hard) at the entry to a turn can create a push and wheel-spin at the exit, causing the car to be loose. If the tires go off, try changing your line. This can be especially effective at the exit of turns. A looser line at the exit (later apex) allows the steering to unwind more, and additional traction at the rear provides acceleration. You may also find more traction in a different groove as the track conditions change.

> **If you have a right front tire go down in a turn, you try to get the car slowed down as much as you can, but you can't use a lot of brake because the car won't turn. If you have a right rear go down you just jam the brakes on because the car is just going to go straight to the wall. But with the front, you've got to slow it down as much as you can without locking the front brakes, so you can keep the car turning, so it will have a better angle at the wall.**
>
> *–Terry Labonte*

A driver needs to watch where the car is placed on the track during cautions. Hot tires pick up debris and used rubber, so stay in the groove. And before a restart, put some heat back into the tires with heavy braking and accelerating, and clean the tires with a swerving motion of the steering. By paying attention to the needs of the tires and the circumstances you are faced with, an effective plan can be put into action to improve traction and increase tire life. What you do with the brakes, throttle, and steering greatly influences what happens at those four little tire contact patches. Use patience and discipline to manage them, and you will be repaid with improved performance and a larger share of the purse.

TIRE TRACTION

Many factors affect tire traction, but we have no control over most of them. Those over which

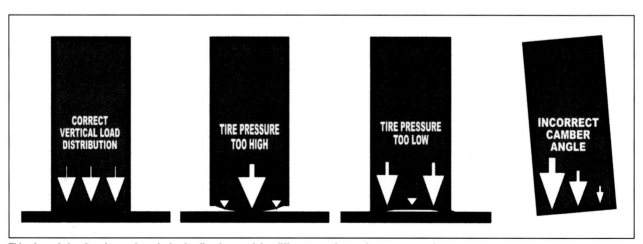

This view of the tire shows the relative loading (arrows) for different camber and pressure settings

we have no control include aspect ratio, sidewall stiffness and construction, rubber compound, ply patterns, and other more esoteric engineering features. We have some control over sidewall spring rates (affected by tire pressures within a very narrow range) and static vertical load (weight percentages). The static vertical load is within a narrow range usually specified by rules. Weight transfer, again within a narrow range, is based on the physical nature of the car design and rubber compound where more than one tire choice is available.

TIRE CONTACT PATCH

All else being equal, a bigger tire contact patch means more traction. For most classes, tire size is dictated by rules. As for classes that allow a range of several tire sizes, bigger is not always faster. Sometimes a wider tire is slower because rolling resistance is increased or the suspension cannot control the tire contact patch effectively. But when the tire size or spec is mandated, the size of the contact patch is very important. If you have not maximized the tire contact patch loading with the track surface, you will not have as much traction as you could. Op-

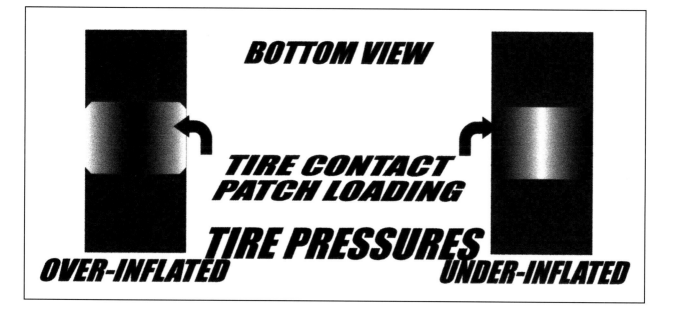

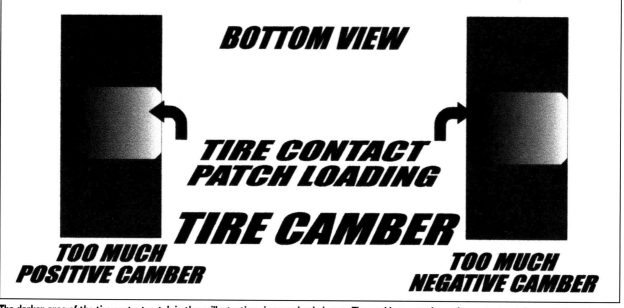

The darker area of the tire contact patch in these illustrations is more loaded area. The goal is to get the entire contact patch equally loaded.

CAMBER GAIN IN BUMP TRAVEL

This illustration shows how camber gain is exhibited during bump or rebound travel.

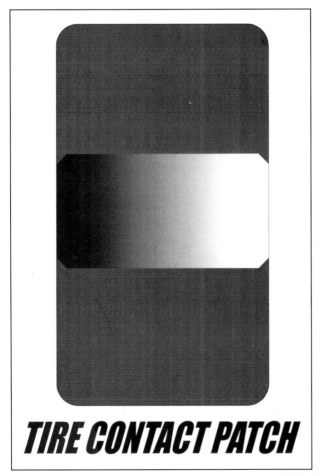

TIRE CONTACT PATCH

GET THE ENTIRE TIRE CONTACT PATCH EQUALLY LOADED

These illustrations show tire loading at the contact patch, with less load being a lighter shade. The goal is to get the load equally distributed across the entire contact patch, as seen on the right. The tire on the left needs a camber adjustment.

timum tire contact patch loading occurs when camber, stagger, and tire pressures are set to optimum. Nearly equal tire temperatures across the surface means that the tire contact patch is equally loaded and doing the maximum amount of work possible. Anything less and you are losing performance.

HOW TIRES MAKE TRACTION

Tires make traction through friction between the rubber molecules at the tire contact patch and the racing surface. Traction increases as vertical load on the tire increases, which is why aerodynamic downforce provides more traction. In addition, most racers understand that the tire will make more traction if the entire contact patch is equally loaded. Thus, monitoring tire temperatures is useful. Misconceptions and misinformation add confusion to an already difficult concept. Let's see if some light can be shed on the topic.

We will not address tire design or construction, since no one I know who races can change those parameters anyway. Let's start with the factors within the tire that affect traction. These are the only factors that affect tire traction:

- **Basic tire design and construction**
- **Sidewall rigidity**
- **Tread rubber compound**
- **Tread design**
- **Tire size**

Most of us run on a spec tire, so none of these factors are under our control. Even if tires are open, the only choices we have are size, compound, and possibly tread design, and those are limited.

We have control over some other factors. These include:

- **Tire pressure**
- **Tire camber**
- **Tire toe in or toe out**
- **Camber change**

Each of these items has an optimum setting that allows the tire to create maximum traction for a given set of circumstances.

It is crucial that we correctly understand vertical load on the tire. Traction increases as the vertical load on the tire increases, but the relationship between vertical load and traction is *not* linear. If the load on the tire is increased, traction does not increase in equal proportion to the load. For example, if the vertical load is doubled, then the traction increase is somewhat less than doubled. If the vertical load is increased by 200 pounds, the traction increase may only be about 175 pounds. At this point, we will explain traction in terms of pounds of force and vertical load on a tire. We'll start with traction.

One way to look at traction is in pounds of force. The most convenient way is to look at the car as an entire unit and measure the force that the tires create. Most racers have heard the term *g-force*. If a car accelerates at 1.0 g, and the car weighs 3,000 pounds, then the tires are producing 3,000 pounds of traction force. This applies to acceleration forward, braking (negative acceleration) and cornering (lateral acceleration). A late-model stock car can produce a cornering force of about 1.4 gs in a flat corner, about 1.25 gs under braking, and somewhere around 0.50 g in acceleration on a short track with a very low final drive ratio. For a 3,000-pound car cornering at 1.4 gs, the traction in pounds is 4,200 pounds (3,000 x 1.4 = 4,200). That is a lot of force from those four tire contact patches.

Vertical load is measured at the tire contact patch. This includes the weight resting on the tire contact patch plus any aerodynamic downforce. If the car creates any aerodynamic lift, then the vertical load on the tire will be less than the weight on the tire, because the car is lifting instead of being pushed down. Aerodynamic downforce is advantageous, because it increases traction without increasing the weight of the car. Let's look more closely at this, since it is another area of some confusion.

Downforce is pretty much a traction freebie. It costs a little in acceleration at high speeds and reduces top speed, but it adds no weight to the car. Adding weight to the car actually reduces the relative amount of traction compared to the total weight of the vehicle. In the previous example, the 3,000 pound car made 4,200 pounds of cornering force at the limit. For example, if 500 pounds are added to the car and nothing else is changed, including the weight distribution, the car will not accelerate as quickly, because it weighs more and the engine is making the same amount of horsepower. It is less obvious that cornering speed will reduce. Here's why. The increase of 500 pounds adds 500 pounds of vertical load to the tires, but because the relationship between the vertical load increase and traction increase is not linear, the amount of traction increase will only be about 400 pounds. The tires now make an additional 560 pounds of trac-

**LEFT TURN DYNAMIC TIRE LOADS
TOO MUCH RIGHT SIDE VERTICAL LOAD**

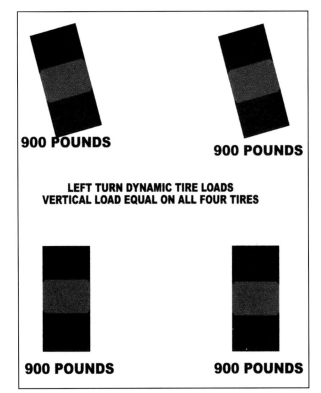

**LEFT TURN DYNAMIC TIRE LOADS
VERTICAL LOAD EQUAL ON ALL FOUR TIRES**

These illustrations show dynamic right-side weight in a turn. The ideal situation is to have all four tires equally loaded in mid-turn, so that all four tire contact patches are doing maximum work. Left-side weight restrictions often make this impossible to achieve.

tion (400 x 1.4) for a total of 4,760 pounds of traction, and a cornering force of only 1.36 gs is achieved. Thus, cornering speed is lost because of the effect on the tires, not on the dynamics of the suspension. This is due entirely to the characteristic of tires where traction does not increase as quickly as load.

The nonlinear relationship also becomes more significant as the design load of the tire is approached. In other words, if a tire has a maximum load capacity of 2,000 pounds, and it normally carries only 750 pounds, doubling the load to 1,500 pounds is approaching the design limit. In this case, the traction may only increase by about half the extra load. If the design load is exceeded, the situation gets worse, and traction decreases. There is nothing you can actually do to a tire or suspension to change this nonlinear relationship, but there are plenty of factors you need to understand in order to minimize its effect and allow your race car to create the maximum possible amount of traction.

These factors are crucial to maximizing traction for each individual tire: camber angle at the front; stagger at the rear; tire pressure; toe settings of the front and rear axle (axle housing squareness, roll steer, and axle squareness at the rear, and bump steer at the front).

The uniform goal in every case is to have the entire tire contact patch equally loaded across the surface of the contact patch. If the entire contact patch is not equally loaded, you are not getting all the traction possible from that tire. If you look at the tire contact patch as a series of 1-inch squares, one square compared to another acts just like one tire compared to another tire. Reducing the load on one square increases the load on another square. The square loosing load loses traction more quickly than the other square gains traction from the increased load. In other words, the tire contact patch as a whole is making less traction than it could be if the contact patch was equally loaded over its entire area. This is hard to achieve, but the team doing the best job has its tires working best.

Once you have the entire tire contact patch at each corner working to its maximum traction potential, then the goal is to get all four tires creating the maximum amount of traction possible for the whole vehicle. Accomplishing this requires an understanding of weight transfer.

TIRE SLIP ANGLE

The tire slip angle, is the amount of twist in the tire sidewall that causes the tire contact patch to turn at a smaller angle than the wheel centerline. The difference between the two is the slip angle which determines the lateral force of the tire. At a given slip angle, the tire will create the maximum cornering force. At a smaller slip angle, the tire will create less cornering force and the same holds true at greater slip angles. The goal for the driver is to keep the tire at the optimum slip angle for maximum cornering force at all times in a corner. This is not an easy task. The front slip angles versus the rear slip angle determine the handling balance of the car. If they are equal, the car is neutral. If the fronts are bigger than the rear, the car will push or understeer. If the rears are greater, the car will be loose or oversteer.

WEIGHT TRANSFER

During cornering, weight transfers from the inside to the outside. Under braking, weight transfers from the rear to the front and under acceleration from the front to the rear. Weight transfer reduces overall vehicle traction. In cornering situations, weight moves off the inside tires to the outside

During braking, weight transfers off the rear tires to the front tires as shown.

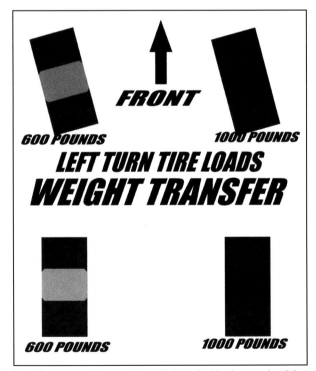

In a left turn, weight transfers off the left side tires to the right side tires as shown.

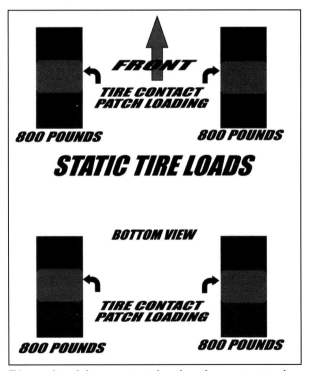

This top view of tire contact patches show the car at rest and the static loads on each tire contact patch.

ACCELERATION TIRE LOADS
WEIGHT TRANSFER

During acceleration, weight transfers off the front tires to the rear tires as shown.

tires. This changes vertical load on all four tires. Two tires (the inside) lose vertical load while the other two gain vertical load. The inside tires lose traction while the outside tires gain traction. Sounds OK so far. But remember that the relationship between vertical load on a tire and the traction force of that tire is not linear. The weight coming off the inside tires causes a loss of traction faster than the outside tires gain traction from the newfound additional vertical load. So the net total traction of the tires is reduced, compared to the same situation if no weight transfer occurred. Since it is not possible to eliminate weight transfer in a corner, we at least want to minimize it so that the overall traction remains as high as possible.

Under braking, the same thing occurs, but is less pronounced. Under acceleration on a rear-drive car, weight transfer actually helps accelerate the car because the drive wheels are gaining traction while the tires losing traction are not driving the car. The opposite is true for a front-wheel drive car. You gain some acceleration traction from more weight transfer. However, if you have to turn and slow down for corners, weight transfer hurts lap times, so our goal is to minimize weight transfer as much as possible.

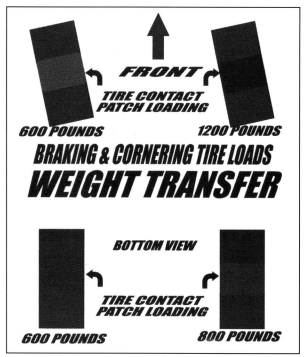

BRAKING & CORNERING TIRE LOADS
WEIGHT TRANSFER

When braking and cornering, weight transfers both forward and to the outside as shown.

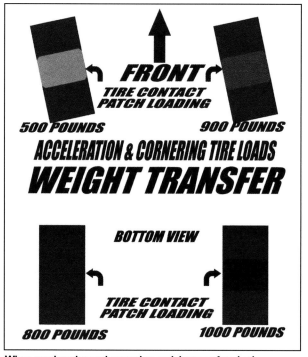

ACCELERATION & CORNERING TIRE LOADS
WEIGHT TRANSFER

When accelerating and cornering, weight transfers both rearward and to the outside as shown.

There are only four factors that effect the amount of weight transferred:

- **The total weight of the vehicle—more weight means more weight transfer, all else being equal.**
- **The force acting on the center of gravity—more force means more weight transfer.**
- **The height of the center of gravity above ground—higher centers of gravity transfer more weight.**
- **The track width (for cornering) or the wheelbase (for acceleration and braking)—narrower track widths or shorter wheelbase mean more weight transfer.**

Let's look a little more closely at each of these. Total weight we have already discussed. Since we want to run as light as possible, or at minimum weight, this is a constant factor that we cannot change unless we are over the weight limit. The traction force of the tires determines the force acting at the center of gravity. Reducing the traction or driving below the limits of tire traction are certainly contrary to our goal of getting around the track as fast as possible, so again, this is not really a factor.

Once each contact patch has equal load distribution, try to get the load equal (equal average tire temperatures) on all four tires.

Maximum track width is always specified by rules. Unless you are running at very high speeds, in which aerodynamic drag is a big factor, you want to run the widest track width possible, so again this will not have a big impact on performance. But the center of gravity, the point within the car where it, if suspended at that point, would be in perfect balance, can be altered. It cannot be drastically altered on some cars, but with most cars, it can be changed enough to affect performance. Simply keeping weight as low as possible in the car will lower the center of gravity, thus reducing weight transfer. This is very important to consider when building a car or adding ballast to the chassis.

There are many misconceptions about weight transfer. Only the four items listed affect the amount of weight transfer. Body roll has a very minimal effect and should not be considered a factor. Dive and squat are not factors. So do not be misled to believe that anything other than the four factors listed above have an effect on the amount of weight transferred while cornering, braking or accelerating.

UNDERSTANDING TIRE TEMPERATURES

At your home track, you're fast, but cannot maintain quite as much cornering speed as your closest competitor. He goes through mid-turn and the exit of the turn just a little bit faster. You've been monitoring tire temperatures all season, and the temps look good. All of the inside temps are just a little hotter than the outside, and the middle temps are right in between. Pressures and camber are dialed, and stagger seems to be working out well. What else can you do?

You know that tire temperatures offer clues about traction at each tire contact patch, but what about comparing one tire, or pair of tires to the others? The average tire temps are another clue you can use to find more traction.

Average tire temperatures are found for each tire by adding the three temp readings together then dividing by 3. In addition to the average temperature at each tire, you need to know the average temperatures for the left side and right side, the front and the rear and the two diagonals. The goal is to get the average temps at each tire as close as possible to each other. This means that each tire is doing as much work as possible. If one tire is much hotter, or cooler, tuning might make

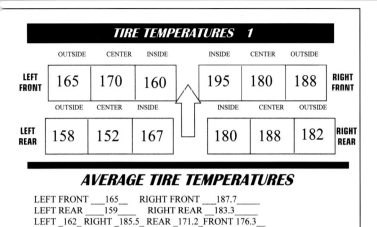

TIRE TEMPERATURES   1

	OUTSIDE	CENTER	INSIDE		INSIDE	CENTER	OUTSIDE	
LEFT FRONT	165	170	160		195	180	188	RIGHT FRONT
	OUTSIDE	CENTER	INSIDE		INSIDE	CENTER	OUTSIDE	
LEFT REAR	158	152	167		180	188	182	RIGHT REAR

AVERAGE TIRE TEMPERATURES

LEFT FRONT ___165__   RIGHT FRONT ___187.7_____
LEFT REAR ____159___   RIGHT REAR __183.3_____
LEFT _162_ RIGHT _185.5_ REAR _171.2_ FRONT 176.3__
RF/LR _173.3___   LF/RR __174.2_____

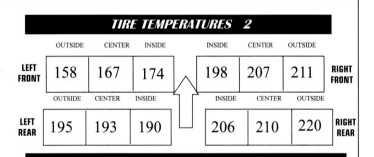

TIRE TEMPERATURES   2

	OUTSIDE	CENTER	INSIDE		INSIDE	CENTER	OUTSIDE	
LEFT FRONT	158	167	174		198	207	211	RIGHT FRONT
	OUTSIDE	CENTER	INSIDE		INSIDE	CENTER	OUTSIDE	
LEFT REAR	195	193	190		206	210	220	RIGHT REAR

AVERAGE TIRE TEMPERATURES

LEFT FRONT ___166.3__   RIGHT FRONT _205.3___
LEFT REAR ____192.7__   RIGHT REAR __212____
LEFT 179.5_ RIGHT _08.7_ REAR 202.3 FRONT 185.8_
RF/LR _199_____   LF/RR __189.2_____

TIRE TEMPERATURES   3

	OUTSIDE	CENTER	INSIDE		INSIDE	CENTER	OUTSIDE	
LEFT FRONT	160	158	156		189	190	197	RIGHT FRONT
	OUTSIDE	CENTER	INSIDE		INSIDE	CENTER	OUTSIDE	
LEFT REAR	170	178	182		190	191	201	RIGHT REAR

AVERAGE TIRE TEMPERATURES

LEFT FRONT __158_____   RIGHT FRONT _192____
LEFT REAR ____176.7_   RIGHT REAR __194____
LEFT _167.3_ RIGHT _193_ REAR _185.3 FRONT _175
RF/LR _184.3_____   LF/RR __176_____

your car faster. It is important for stock car drivers to have a basic understanding of tuning the chassis, especially with tire temperatures.

What average tire temperature clues can tell you is the effectiveness of static weight distribution, how crossweight is affecting the car, if the roll couple distribution is in the ballpark, brake balance, how the driver is using the controls, and if there may be chassis alignment problems.

Always look at the individual temps because they will still tell you how well that tire contact patch is working on the track surface. Use the individual temps to tune pressures first, then camber at the front and stagger at the rear.

Here are some examples of tire temps and their interpretation.

Tire Temperature Chart 1

This chart shows pressures that are not correct. The right front pressure is too low, the left front is too high, the left rear is too low, and the right rear is too high. It takes practice to determine how much to change the pressure for a given set of conditions. The greater the difference, the greater the change needs to be to get the contact patch flat on the race track. Keep in mind that when the center temp is hotter, the pressure is too high, and if the center temp is cooler, the pressure is too low.

Tire Temperature Chart 2

The front camber is off in this chart. At the left front, the wheel needs more positive camber to heat the outside edge of the tire (which is on the inside of the turn). The right front needs more

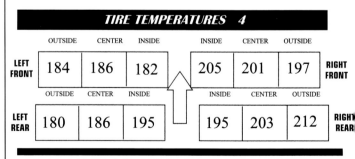

TIRE TEMPERATURES   4

	OUTSIDE	CENTER	INSIDE		INSIDE	CENTER	OUTSIDE	
LEFT FRONT	184	186	182		205	201	197	RIGHT FRONT
	OUTSIDE	CENTER	INSIDE		INSIDE	CENTER	OUTSIDE	
LEFT REAR	180	186	195		195	203	212	RIGHT REAR

AVERAGE TIRE TEMPERATURES

LEFT FRONT _184_____   RIGHT FRONT _201___
LEFT REAR _187_____   RIGHT REAR _203.3___
LEFT 185.5_ RIGHT 202.2_ REAR 195.2 FRONT 192.5
RF/LR _194_____   LF/RR _193.7_____

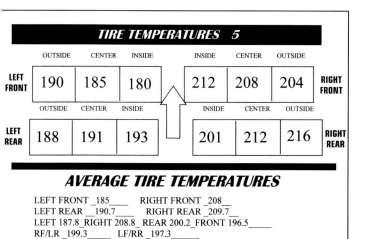

TIRE TEMPERATURES 5

LEFT FRONT	OUTSIDE	CENTER	INSIDE		INSIDE	CENTER	OUTSIDE	RIGHT FRONT
	190	185	180		212	208	204	
LEFT REAR	OUTSIDE	CENTER	INSIDE		INSIDE	CENTER	OUTSIDE	RIGHT REAR
	188	191	193		201	212	216	

AVERAGE TIRE TEMPERATURES

LEFT FRONT _185____   RIGHT FRONT _208__
LEFT REAR __190.7____   RIGHT REAR _209.7__
LEFT 187.8_RIGHT 208.8_ REAR 200.2_FRONT 196.5____
RF/LR _199.3____   LF/RR _197.3_____

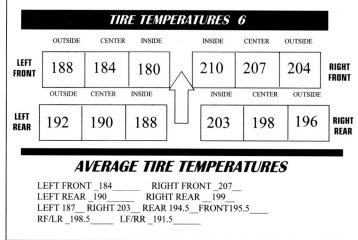

TIRE TEMPERATURES 6

LEFT FRONT	OUTSIDE	CENTER	INSIDE		INSIDE	CENTER	OUTSIDE	RIGHT FRONT
	188	184	180		210	207	204	
LEFT REAR	OUTSIDE	CENTER	INSIDE		INSIDE	CENTER	OUTSIDE	RIGHT REAR
	192	190	188		203	198	196	

AVERAGE TIRE TEMPERATURES

LEFT FRONT _184_____   RIGHT FRONT _207__
LEFT REAR _190_____   RIGHT REAR __199__
LEFT 187__ RIGHT 203__ REAR 194.5__FRONT195.5____
RF/LR _198.5____   LF/RR _191.5_____

negative camber. Since tires make the most traction in a corner with a small amount of dynamic negative camber (that's negative camber while cornering), the inside edge of the right front and the outside edge of the left front should show temps between 5 and 10 degrees hotter than the outside edge. This indicates that the tires are achieving maximum traction.

Tire Temperature Chart 3

Look at the rear tire temps here. The right edges of the rear tires are hotter than the left edges. This car would be faster with more stagger, or some camber in the rear axle housing.

Tire Temperature Chart 4

Look at the front tire temps, which are nearly perfect at first glance. This temperature pattern can be caused by too much toe-out at the front. Although the camber appears to be correct, it could be off, costing tire traction, but the excessive toe out masks the real problem. For this reason, it is important to routinely check toe. A slight bump or wear can change toe settings and hide other problems.

Tire Temperature Chart 5

Roll steer, or rear axle steer, can cause temperature patterns like those shown here. It looks as if the car needs more stagger, but the rear suspension links could cause the rear axle to move forward or backward at the right side wheel. This causes scrub and heats the leading edge of the tire contact patch. Even though the average temperatures show that the car should be loose, this car probably pushes. The most important thing is

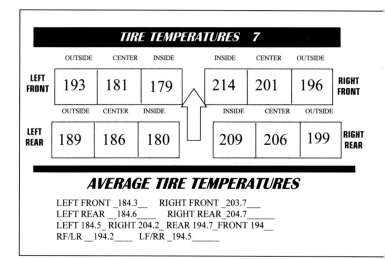

TIRE TEMPERATURES 7

LEFT FRONT	OUTSIDE	CENTER	INSIDE		INSIDE	CENTER	OUTSIDE	RIGHT FRONT
	193	181	179		214	201	196	
LEFT REAR	OUTSIDE	CENTER	INSIDE		INSIDE	CENTER	OUTSIDE	RIGHT REAR
	189	186	180		209	206	199	

AVERAGE TIRE TEMPERATURES

LEFT FRONT _184.3__   RIGHT FRONT _203.7___
LEFT REAR __184.6____   RIGHT REAR 204.7_____
LEFT 184.5_ RIGHT 204.2_ REAR 194.7_FRONT 194__
RF/LR __194.2____   LF/RR _194.5_____

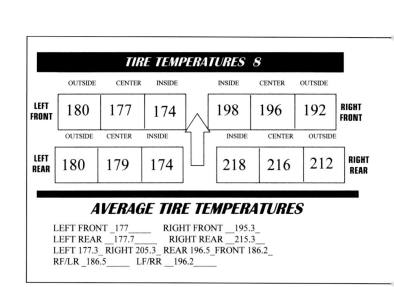

TIRE TEMPERATURES 8

LEFT FRONT	OUTSIDE	CENTER	INSIDE		INSIDE	CENTER	OUTSIDE	RIGHT FRONT
	180	177	174		198	196	192	
LEFT REAR	OUTSIDE	CENTER	INSIDE		INSIDE	CENTER	OUTSIDE	RIGHT REAR
	180	179	174		218	216	212	

AVERAGE TIRE TEMPERATURES

LEFT FRONT _177_____   RIGHT FRONT __195.3_
LEFT REAR __177.7____   RIGHT REAR __215.3__
LEFT 177.3_ RIGHT 205.3_ REAR 196.5_FRONT 186.2_
RF/LR _186.5_____   LF/RR __196.2_____

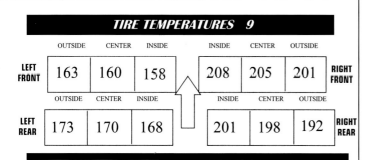

TIRE TEMPERATURES 9

	OUTSIDE	CENTER	INSIDE		INSIDE	CENTER	OUTSIDE	
LEFT FRONT	163	160	158		208	205	201	**RIGHT FRONT**
	OUTSIDE	CENTER	INSIDE		INSIDE	CENTER	OUTSIDE	
LEFT REAR	173	170	168		201	198	192	**RIGHT REAR**

AVERAGE TIRE TEMPERATURES

LEFT FRONT _160.3____   RIGHT FRONT _204.7___
LEFT REAR __170.3____   RIGHT REAR _197_____
LEFT 165.3_ RIGHT 200.3_ REAR 183.7_FRONT 182.5__
RF/LR __187.5____   LF/RR _178.7__

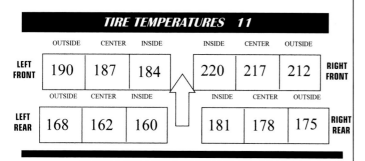

TIRE TEMPERATURES 10

	OUTSIDE	CENTER	INSIDE		INSIDE	CENTER	OUTSIDE	
LEFT FRONT	175	172	170		189	185	180	**RIGHT FRONT**
	OUTSIDE	CENTER	INSIDE		INSIDE	CENTER	OUTSIDE	
LEFT REAR	190	188	182		206	201	197	**RIGHT REAR**

AVERAGE TIRE TEMPERATURES

LEFT FRONT _172.3____   RIGHT FRONT __184.7_
LEFT REAR __186.7____   RIGHT REAR __201.3__
LEFT 179.5_ RIGHT 193__ REAR 194_FRONT 178.5_
RF/LR __185.7____   LF/RR _186.8___

TIRE TEMPERATURES   11

	OUTSIDE	CENTER	INSIDE		INSIDE	CENTER	OUTSIDE	
LEFT FRONT	190	187	184		220	217	212	**RIGHT FRONT**
	OUTSIDE	CENTER	INSIDE		INSIDE	CENTER	OUTSIDE	
LEFT REAR	168	162	160		181	178	175	**RIGHT REAR**

AVERAGE TIRE TEMPERATURES

LEFT FRONT _187____   RIGHT FRONT _216.3__
LEFT REAR __163.3____   RIGHT REAR __178___
LEFT 175.2_ RIGHT 197.2_ REAR 170.7_FRONT 201.7_
RF/LR __189.8____   LF/RR _182.5_____

to not be fooled by the data. You need to know what the rear suspension is doing, so you can make better judgments about the setup.

Tire Temperature Chart 6

This situation shows nearly perfect stagger. It could also occur when the rear axle steers too much, and too little or too much stagger is present. It depends which way the right rear wheel moves during body roll. Avoid letting the data fool you.

Tire Temperature Chart 7

Suspension setup and heat distribution on this chart are close, except the left side weight is too low for optimum cornering load distribution. At all four corners, tire pressures are too low. This is combined with too much front camber and too much stagger at the rear. Combined pressure and stagger/camber problems can be hard to read. The key is that the right edge of the contact patches is closer to the center temperature than the left edge of the contact patch. This indicates a combination of problems, so look closely at tire temperatures to properly interpret them.

Tire Temperature Chart 8

In this situation, average tire temperatures can really be helpful. Left side and right side averages look really good. The rear average is higher, indicating a push condition. Look at the diagonal averages. The left front/right rear average is hotter than the opposite, which often indicates that the car has too little crossweight. Combined with the rear average showing a push, the car would likely respond well to a higher crossweight percentage. The right front/left rear diagonal usually runs hotter on asphalt especially with radial tires. The opposite is usually true on dirt. Keep in mind that many factors must be considered. The average temps are indicators, not hard, fast rules.

Tire Temperature Chart 9

Rules often dictate left-side weight percentages, but it is important to run with the maximum left-side weight, especially on asphalt or dry, slick dirt. Look at the left-side average versus the right-side. More left-side weight would put more heat in the left side tires, meaning the left-side tires are working more and the car can corner faster, since all four tires are doing more work.

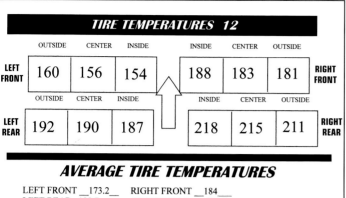

TIRE TEMPERATURES 12

	OUTSIDE	CENTER	INSIDE		INSIDE	CENTER	OUTSIDE	
LEFT FRONT	160	156	154		188	183	181	RIGHT FRONT
	OUTSIDE	CENTER	INSIDE		INSIDE	CENTER	OUTSIDE	
LEFT REAR	192	190	187		218	215	211	RIGHT REAR

AVERAGE TIRE TEMPERATURES

LEFT FRONT __173.2__   RIGHT FRONT __184__
LEFT REAR _189.7____   RIGHT REAR ___214.7_
LEFT 173.2_ RIGHT 199.3_ REAR 202.2 FRONT 170.3_
RF/LR _186.8_____   LF/RR _185.6_____

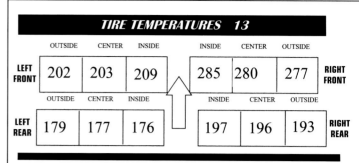

TIRE TEMPERATURES 13

	OUTSIDE	CENTER	INSIDE		INSIDE	CENTER	OUTSIDE	
LEFT FRONT	202	203	209		285	280	277	RIGHT FRONT
	OUTSIDE	CENTER	INSIDE		INSIDE	CENTER	OUTSIDE	
LEFT REAR	179	177	176		197	196	193	RIGHT REAR

AVERAGE TIRE TEMPERATURES

LEFT FRONT _204.7____   RIGHT FRONT __280.7_
LEFT REAR __177.3____   RIGHT REAR __195.3___
LEFT 191_ RIGHT 238_ REAR 186.3_FRONT 242.7__
RF/LR __229__   LF/RR __200____

Tire Temperature Chart 10

The rear average temperatures are hotter. This indicates the possibility of too little rear weight percentage. With less traction at the rear, the rear tires are prone to spinning as you come off the corners, and this puts more heat in the rear tires.

Tire Temperature Chart 11

The front tire average is 31 degrees hotter than the rear average, shows a push, and indicates that the front roll couple percentage is too high. In other words, the front has too much roll resistance. The front springs could be softened. But a softer front sway bar (anti-roll bar) would be a better choice, because it will not change the control of the tire contact patch over bumps. In this case, a stiffer rear sway bar (if the car is equipped with one) or stiffer rear spring is the best choice. The reason to change the rear instead of the front is that the front average tire temps are at the optimum temperature while the rear averages are cooler than optimum. The stiffer rear setup will put more load on the rear tires.

Tire Temperature Chart 12

This is the opposite situation from Chart 11. In this case, the front bar could be stiffened a little, or the rear springs lowered a little, since all of the tires are within a good operating range.

Tire Temperature Chart 13

We looked at the traction circle and how it relates to the driver's use of the controls. This is a case of extreme understeer, or push. In this case, the driver has applied too much brake for

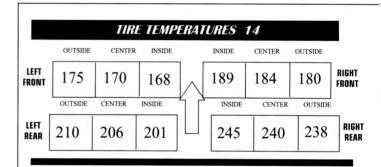

TIRE TEMPERATURES 14

	OUTSIDE	CENTER	INSIDE		INSIDE	CENTER	OUTSIDE	
LEFT FRONT	175	170	168		189	184	180	RIGHT FRONT
	OUTSIDE	CENTER	INSIDE		INSIDE	CENTER	OUTSIDE	
LEFT REAR	210	206	201		245	240	238	RIGHT REAR

AVERAGE TIRE TEMPERATURES

LEFT FRONT _171____   RIGHT FRONT __184.3__
LEFT REAR __205.7____   RIGHT REAR ___241__
LEFT 188.3_ RIGHT 212.7_ REAR 223.3_FRONT177.6_
RF/LR _195___   LF/RR _206__

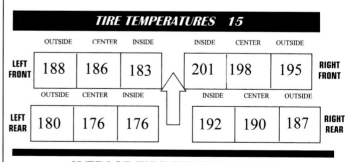

TIRE TEMPERATURES 15

	OUTSIDE	CENTER	INSIDE		INSIDE	CENTER	OUTSIDE	
LEFT FRONT	188	186	183		201	198	195	RIGHT FRONT
	OUTSIDE	CENTER	INSIDE		INSIDE	CENTER	OUTSIDE	
LEFT REAR	180	176	176		192	190	187	RIGHT REAR

AVERAGE TIRE TEMPERATURES

LEFT FRONT __185.7____   RIGHT FRONT _198___
LEFT REAR __176.7___   RIGHT REAR __189.7___
LEFT 181.2_ RIGHT 193.8_ REAR 183.2 FRONT 191.8_
RF/LR _187.3_____   LF/RR __187.7_____

the amount of steering lock being used, and the situation only gets worse in mid-turn and at the exit as the throttle is applied, still with too much steering lock for the amount the other controls are being used.

Tire Temperature Chart 14

This is a case that looks like an extremely loose condition, but the car was neutral. The real problem was far too much rear brake bias. The master cylinders had been reversed, making adjustments ineffective.

Tire Temperature Chart 15

When you see temps like these, and you know that all the settings are dialed, sit back and smile. You have achieved a really sound setup. Now work to keep it that way.

TEN CHASSIS TUNING TRICKS USING TIRE TEMPERATURES

Your race car is perfectly balanced through the corners. It gets into the turns quickly, and corner exit is strong, but you consistently lose two car lengths in mid-turn. Toe is correct, stagger is correct, crossweights seem right. What could cause the car to be slow in mid-turn? The answer is a lack of total traction.

The goal when you set up your race car is to get maximum traction as well as create a good balance all the way around the race track. If, for some reason, maximum traction is not there, the car will not perform to its peak at some point on the race track. One of the most important jobs a race team has is to get the maximum traction possible out of the tires. And the driver must have a basic understanding of the process to really develop skills as a driver. Here are a few tricks to help you accomplish that goal.

1. Consider All Four Tires

The goal is to get the most traction possible from all four tires. The harder each tire works, the more traction the car will have. Thus, the car will enter, get through and exit the corners faster. One sign of how hard a tire is working (and therefore the tire's traction) is the average temperature of the tire. If the average temperature is higher than the maximum temperature for your tires, that tire is working too hard. If the average temperature is lower than the average temperature of the other tires, then that tire is not working hard enough and your car will not perform at its optimum. The colder tire needs to work harder, and you need to figure out how to do that.

Comparing average tire temperatures can offer a wealth of information. The cold tire needs to

If the driver accelerates too quickly, the car will lose traction (1), or it will become very loose (2).

If the car carries too much speed entering the corner (1), the car will lose traction and slide up the track (2).

work harder. The hotter end of the car is losing traction before the colder end. If the rear average temp is hotter than the front, the car is loose; if the front average is hotter, the car is pushing. This could indicate a change in roll couple distribution (spring rates or sway bar rates, or both). If the outside average tire temperature is hotter than the inside, more static weight on the inside would help, assuming rules allow more static weight. More static left side weight means that the left-to-right weights in a corner (dynamic weight distribution) are closer and the vertical load on each tire is closer to equal. Diagonal average tire temps will offer clues about stagger and crossweights for a given situation.

2. Look at the Complete Tire Contact Patch

Where the average tire temperature for a given tire provides a good comparison for overall traction, the individual tire temperatures at a given tire offer solid information about what is happening at each tire contact patch. Comparing individual tire temperatures at a given tire can tell you how to tune that tire. If an edge of a tire is hotter, the camber is off. If the middle of the tire is hotter or colder, the pressure is off.

3. Always Take Tire Temperatures

Tire temps are the only link you have to what is happening at the tire contact patch. You need to know what is happening, so always take tire temps, even after a race.

4. Take Tire Temperatures at Different Locations on the Race Track

The habit is take tire temps in the pits. On a test day, you may be able to take tire temps at any point on the race track. This can give you important information about what the tires are doing under a variety of conditions. For example, if you measure temps coming off a corner, you will see how the tires are working at this critical point on the track. Naturally, the rear tires should be hotter in this situation, just as the fronts should be hotter under hard braking. You should keep these facts in mind when taking tire temps at various points.

When you stop to take temps, slow gently or too much heat will build in the front tires, unless you are measuring corner entry temps. When you

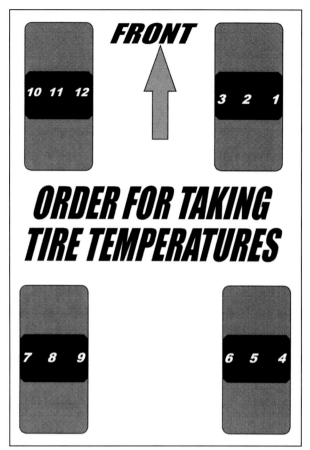

This illustration shows the order in which tire temperatures should be taken.

analyze temps, take into account where you took the temps. Mid-turn setup is best when all tire temps are close to equal. Fronts temps should be hotter at corner entry, but as close to equal left to right as possible. Rears should be equal, but hotter than fronts at corner exit.

5. Work Fast

When you take tire temps, work fast. Tire temps equalize quickly, and tires cool quickly, so fast temp taking will give you better results. If you are short handed, hand the driver a note pad and have the driver write the temps down while the crew reads them.

6. Be Consistent

Always take temps the same way every time. Start at the same tire, and always start at either the inside or outside of the tire. Take temps in the same order around the car. Keep in mind that the last temp taken will not be as accurate as the first

If possible, one should take tire temperatures on the track. This illustration designates ideal spots for taking tire temperature readings on the race track.

because the last tire will have had more time to cool and to equalize. Its a good idea to take the first tire temp over after the last one to get an idea about how much the last tire has cooled and equalized. Always record pressures after temps also.

7. Pay Attention to Static Weight Distribution

One way to get average temps closer together, and to increase total traction, is to look at the temps and compare them to static weight distribution. If a tire is more than 15 to 20 degrees cooler, that tire needs more static weight on it. This is likely an inside tire, and usually the front. More static weight on a cold tire means more dynamic weight on the same tire while cornering, and less on another tire. This will most often improve overall traction, although handling balance may need to be reestablished.

8. Dynamic Weight Distribution Is Key

The goal is to have dynamic weight distribution as equal as possible at each tire during a corner, and more weight on the rear coming off the turns. We can calculate dynamic weight distribution, and we can use load sensors to actually measure dynamic weight distribution. However, these are difficult or expensive options. Tire temps can give the same basic information, and allow you to make good judgments about improving setup.

9. Heat in the Tires Tells the Story

If the tire has heat, it's making traction, up to the point that the tire gets too hot. When all the tires are in the optimum range of operating temperature, you are getting maximum traction. Anything less than that indicates your race car could be getting around the track faster. Here are some important facts to keep in mind.

Rusty Wallace contemplates the setup of his Pontiac Grand Prix at the 1993 Winston race. Each team constantly searches for the best tire and suspension combination for a particular track. Often, the setup changes made during the final pit stop of the race determine the winner.

If any tire is overheated, it is doing too much work. A change is needed. If all tires are overheated, the compound may be too soft for the car and conditions. If front tires are overheating, it may that the driver is using the brakes too hard while steering.

If the rear tires are overheating, the driver may be using too much throttle exiting the corners, causing wheel spin. If temps are too cool overall, it could be the ambient weather conditions. If it's cold, take that into account. If average temps are too cold, it could be the driver. If the driver is not up to speed, temps will never get to optimum and handling problems should be nearly nonexistent. The driver needs to push the car closer to the limits of traction before any setup issue can be resolved with any clarity.

10. Put Heat Where You Need It

If a tire is colder than the rest, figure out how to get more heat there. Here are some tips. Start with static weight distribution. Put weight on the cold tire.

If the front or rear is colder, put more roll couple distribution (stiffer springs/bars) at that end. If the diagonal average temperatures are off, play with stagger and crossweights to put heat in the colder diagonal.

Toe and bump steer can be used to get heat in the inside front tire.

What happens at the tire contact patch is all we really care about when trying to get the maximum traction from a race car. Nothing else really matters. Tire temperatures are the easiest and most cost-effective link you have to the action at the tire contact patch. Using the tire temperatures effectively can pay considerable dividends on the race track. Understanding what the temps mean is one of the skills every stock car driver needs.

How the Suspension Affects Handling

While a stock car driver does not need to be a suspension engineer, a basic understanding of how the various suspension components affect the handling is both important and useful. So often chassis adjustments are made without a clear understanding of what is going on. Drivers are the worst culprits in this scenario. A driver should not make changes because someone else did or it was recommended as the way to be fast or win races. Make changes based on what the car needs to go fast.

CAMBER

Camber is the tilt of a front tire when viewed from the front. Camber is positive if the top of the tire is tilted to the outside; negative if the tilt is to the inside. Since most front suspension systems gain positive camber during bump (compression) travel, and the outside tire goes into bump during cornering, some amount of negative camber is needed to offset the camber gain and keep the tire contact patch flat on the road surface during cornering.

Camber gain is caused by the front suspension geometry. During body roll, the outside front tire gains camber. This tilts the tire contact patch and changes the loading across the tread and reduces traction. Some static negative camber can compensate for this,

The Woods Brothers team works on the shocks of the No. 21 Citco-sponsored Ford Thunderbird. It's vital for the team to find the best shock valving and spring setup for each track the team visits, so the car accelerates and handles at its maximum potential. *Nigel Kinrade*

These illustrations show the various camber settings of the front suspension system.

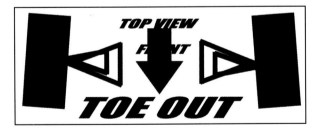

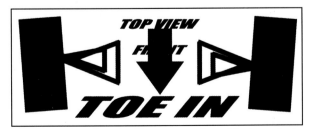

These illustrations show the different toe settings of the front wheels.

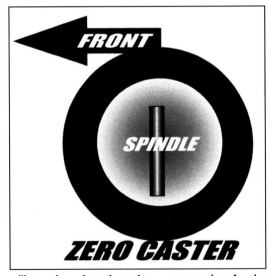

These illustrations show the various caster settings for the front suspension.

but too much negative camber causes accelerated tire wear and hurts straight line braking performance. Stiffer front spring and anti-roll bars reduce body roll, which reduces bump travel and camber gain. This reduces the amount of static negative camber needed to keep the tire contact patch flat on the road surface in a corner.

TOE

Toe is the angle of the front tires when viewed from above. Toe-in means the fronts of the tires are closer together than the rear of the tires. Toe-out is the opposite. Cars will turn into a corner better with a small amount of toe-out. Toe-out is nearly always used in stock car racing. More is used on short tracks, less on speedways. Too much toe-out causes excessive heat build-up on the inside edge of the tire contact patch. Excessive toe-out also causes drag and reduced straightline stability, a negative on a speedway.

CASTER

Caster is the angle of the steering axis at the front of the car when viewed from the side (see illustration). More caster increases the self-centering effect of the steering, but also increases tire scrub slightly while cornering. Caster angles different from left to right cause the steering to pull in one direction. This is called caster stagger. Some caster stagger is used on stock cars. The amount is mostly driver preference.

SPRINGS

The job of the springs is first to keep the car from bottoming, second to allow the tire contact patches to stay on the track surface over bumps, and finally to partially control body roll. Stiffer springs can allow a car to have a lower ride height and also reduce body roll, both important for improved handling. On the other side, stiffer springs reduce the ability of the tire contact patch to stay on the road surface over bumps, hurting traction and increasing ride harshness. Springs must be designed to be a compromise for a given set of conditions.

ANTI-ROLL BARS (SWAY BARS)

Anti-roll bars serve two purposes. First, they are intended to control body roll so that camber gain is not excessive. Second, the bars are a convenient way to balance the front-to- rear roll resistance to achieve the best handling balance. Roll re-

The camber angle on this front tire is typical of a stock car. The goal is to get the tire working all the way across the tread surface. Tire temperatures will tell us how well this has been accomplished

sistance is a combination of resistance provided by springs and anti-roll bars. The amount of total roll resistance at the front divided by total roll resistance front and rear is a percentage called "roll couple distribution." Both of these can be affected with springs, but to really control body roll with springs would require springs too stiff for control over bumpy surfaces.

SHOCKS

The shock absorber is one of the most complex parts affecting the handling of a race car. To become a skilled stock car racer, you must understand how shocks work and how they affect handling. Those topics will be covered in this chapter.

Shock absorbers dampen vibrations of the wheels and the chassis when bumps and ruts are encountered or during weight transfer. We've all seen cars bouncing down the road after hitting a bump. The shocks have lost dampening capacity and cannot control spring oscillations. Shock absorbers actually dampen that vibration and for this reason really should be called dampers.

The shock absorber works in conjunction with the spring to control movement of the suspension and chassis. The springs absorb force of bumps and control body roll. The shocks control the oscillations of the springs, determining how fast the spring compresses or extends. Stiffer shock rates slow spring movements, and a softer shock rate al-

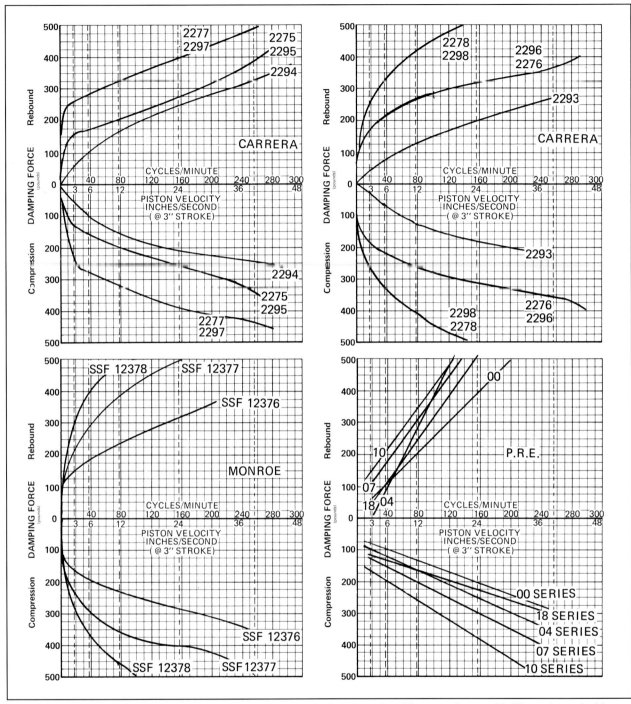

These shock absorber dyno graphs show a variety of shocks in bump and rebound travel at different settings or with different internal valving to change the rates. Different rates are used to change either transient handling response in corners (low shaft speeds), or tire control over bumps (medium to high shaft speeds). By correlating the graphs to on-track performance, teams can find the best combinations and make them repeatable when they return to that track, or find similar circumstances at other tracks.

lows a faster spring movement. A shock is way too soft if it allows the springs to oscillate, or bounce, more than one full cycle. A shock is way too stiff if the shock limits suspension travel. A shock and spring that are too stiff can cause the tire contact patch to bounce off the road surface over bumps, or jack weight in the car after body roll occurs, even pulling the tire off the track surface for an instant.

BUMPS

The first job of a shock is to control the tire contact patch over bumps. In racing, a shock that is too soft allows the chassis to bounce after hitting a bump or rut. In this situation, traction varies over a bump and the car wallows. If the shock is too stiff for a particular track or conditions, the tire contact patch can be pulled of the track surface when a bump is encountered or at least the load on that tire is reduced significantly. This affects handling balance and jacks weight around the chassis, making the car feel unpredictable. When traction is suddenly lost, it is very difficult for the driver to control the car and predict its response. Over bumps, the car feels as if it skates. Since the tire can completely lose contact with the track, this can be a potentially dangerous condition.

COMPRESSION AND REBOUND

Compression dampening is defined as the shock shaft moving toward the top of the shock body. Compression is a result of contacting the front of a bump, the back of a rut, the right- side when turning left, the left-side shocks when exiting a left turn, the front under braking, and the rear under acceleration.

Rebound, or extension, occurs when the shaft is being pulled from the body. This occurs on backside of a bump, the front of a rut, the left side shocks in a left turn, the right side shocks exiting a left turn, the front under acceleration, and the rear under braking.

A shock dampens vibrations by creating friction. Racing shocks all use hydraulic fluid in a tube with a piston. The piston pushes the fluid through a series of valves and bleed holes. The amount of valving determines how fast or slow the piston travels through the hydraulic fluid. Thus, the valving determines the "rate" of the shock. The valves (or shim stack) and bleeds can be varied to change the rate, and different valves and bleeds are used

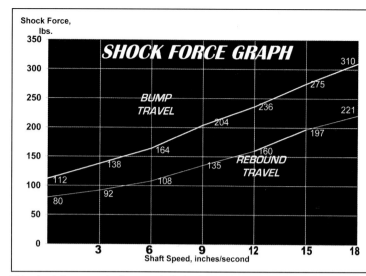

This shock force graph shows typical shock forces in bump and rebound at increasing shaft speeds.

for rebound and compression. The valves for either rebound or compression can be changed, together or independently, to change how the shock valving works over bumps or during body roll and pitch under braking and acceleration.

There are several types of shock designs, but all have the same affect on the chassis. Some shocks are gas charged and some are not. When selecting shocks, a racer should look at quality of materials, wear characteristics, rebuilding, and performance as heat builds up inside the shock.

SHAFT SPEEDS

The speed at which the shaft travels through the fluid in the shock body governs the rate of the shock in both compression and rebound. Shock absorbers are speed sensitive. By using different

The shock absorber on the top is fully extended, or in full rebound travel. The middle shock is fully compressed, or in full bump travel. The shock on the bottom is in the middle of its stroke, where it would be at static ride height.

valves and bleeds, damping rates and shaft speed change. The faster the piston or shaft speed, the stiffer the shock is. Shocks work mostly within a range of about 3 inches per second to about 20 inches per second. The lower speeds come into play during weight transfer, when tire loads are changing. The higher speeds come into play over bumps and ruts. A shock manufacturer can alter low, medium, and high speed valving to control what the shock does in different situations. Low and medium speed valving are used to control the way the shock influences handling. By altering shock valving for different shaft speed ranges, a shock builder or engineer can create a shock that affects tire contact patch control over bumps and ruts and also affects the weight transfer characteristics so that handling can be fine-tuned for a variety of conditions. Bigger open-wheel teams have a wide variety of shocks in the trailer to accommodate a variety of track conditions from both a tire contact patch control perspective (medium to high speed valving) and a handling perspective (low to medium speed valving). The first factor affects overall tire traction, the second affects handling balance at different spots on the race track.

FOUR COMPONENTS OF WEIGHT TRANSFER

How much weight is transferred from one part of the car to another depends on the weight of the car, the track width and wheelbase, the center of gravity height, and the cornering force.

The spring rates, acting at the tire contact patch and influenced by geometric effects from such components as the Panhard bar dictate where the weight is transferred..

When weight is transferred is controlled by the driver's use of the controls: the steering, the brakes, and accelerator.

How fast weight is transferred is determined by the shock rates and the speed at which the driver uses the controls.

HOW SHOCKS AFFECT HANDLING

As we just discussed, the shock controls how fast weight is transferred. This affects the load on a tire and can change the handling balance while weight is being transferred. Once all weight has been transferred, the shock no longer influences handling. When going into a corner, as long as the driver is moving either the steering wheel or the

brake pedal, the shock has an influence on tire loading. Braking causes weight to transfer forward, compressing the front suspension and shocks, extending the rear suspension and shocks. When cornering, the weight transfers from the inside to the outside, extending the inside suspension and shocks while compressing the outside suspension and shocks. When both braking and cornering take place simultaneously, as they nearly always do going into a short track turn, both longitudinal and lateral effects occur. The right front, which is compressing both from roll and pitch, and the left rear, which is extending from both factors, are moving the most and will have the biggest influence. The left front and right rear are receiving opposite movements from roll and pitch, reducing their movement and therefore their influence.

In mid-corner, the longitudinal forces (braking and acceleration) are small, and lateral forces (cornering) are highest. Each shock influences handling in this situation, but shock travel is very small, especially on solid axle cars, which have high roll centers and a small amount of body roll. This reduces the influence of the shock on handling balance.

At the exit, the opposite of corner entry occurs. Under acceleration, the rear shocks go into compression and the fronts into rebound. As cornering is reduced, the inside shocks go into compression and the outside shocks into rebound. While both forces occur in the exit phase of the corner, the left rear and right front move the most. Those shocks have forces working in the same direction, while the left front and right rear have opposing forces. This does not mean that the left front and right rear shocks do not influence handling. The influence is just a little less.

PUSH CONDITION

A slight push going into the corners, as in our example, keeps the driver from going in as deep the other car. Keep in mind, this is a very slight push. The car has a very good basic setup and is very fast. The car ahead is about 1/10th of second a lap faster. Shocks can be very helpful in this situation.

Under hard braking and some cornering, the right front is the most heavily loaded tire on most cars. A push means the front tires are exceeding optimum traction limits. We need a little more traction on the front, and little less on the rear. A big change could make the car loose entering the corner. Or changing the springs, shocks, or torsion bar could upset the perfect balance of the car on the exit.

In this case, going to the left rear or right front shock would have an effect. Stiffer rebound on the left rear or left front, or softer compression damping on the right front will get weight off the rear and onto the right front more quickly. Reducing the left front rebound damping is the least useful change, because that will take the load of the left front more quickly, and this will slightly reduce traction. The softer compression damping right front is a good change, but the best is the left rear rebound. The left rear in many cases, if not most, has more travel in this situation than any other shock, so a stiffer left rear rebound is the best change to make, since it is likely to be most effective.

A stiffer rebound setting on the left rear will help the entry push problem. Let's say we go one number or click stiffer in both bump and rebound. We want the stiffer rebound, but what will the stiffer compression valving on the left rear do to the handling? The stiffer compression on the left rear could cause the car to loosen up at the exit. If it helps going in, it will likely loosen the car on the exit. Since the exit is more important than the entry for faster lap times, this may not be an advantageous change.

In most cases, this car is really good except for one spot in a corner. One option is to use a shock with adjustable rebound settings or to use a split valve shock. Another option is to have a shock custom valved for your particular application. In our example, increasing the rebound valving one number with the compression valving remaining the same cures the entry push without changing the balance in mid-turn or on the exit. And the goal is to maintain maximum traction and the best balance. But if the push were bigger, this change may help a little, but it would not cure the problem. Something else would be causing the problem.

Let's look at one more example. In this case, the car is loose on the exit. Again a shock change will only help if the car is close to its ideal setup. In this scenario, the driver is spinning the rear tires under acceleration, which is especially likely on a slick track, and this could cause the problem. A shock change should provide better traction, but will not cure the problem. In this case we could decrease the left rear compression or decrease the right front re-

bound. Decreasing the right front rebound allows the weight to get off that corner faster, which would help the most, but the left rear compression reduction would be nearly as good. Again, adjustable shocks or split valve shocks will help here.

HOW THE DRIVER AFFECTS SHOCK BEHAVIOR

The rate or speed of driver inputs on the controls directly affects how the shocks perform. For example, very fast steering wheel movements cause the body to roll faster and change the shaft speed of the shocks. This changes the rate of the shock and affects handling by changing the rate of weight transfer. This can be compounded by the fact that the driver is most often using more than one control at a time. How fast the driver turns the steering wheel and how fast the driver pushes on the brake pedal has a big affect on the handling going into a corner. It is for this reason that the driver must be smooth in using the controls. Abrupt steering or pedal applications can affect the handling in a negative way, and it can be very tough to tune the chassis to overcome this. On the other hand, a driver can use abrupt techniques on the controls to overcome handling ills. This can be beneficial during a race when the chassis cannot be altered to cure a problem.

SPLIT VALVE AND ADJUSTABLE SHOCKS

Split valve shocks contain different compression or rebound valving than a typical shock.

The black rubber on the shaft not only cleans the shaft, but can be used to get a basic idea of bump travel at that corner of the car.

Chassis tuning with these shocks allows specific handling problems to be cured by changing one or more shocks. Adjustable shocks can offer adjustments in rebound only or for both compression and rebound (double adjustable). Tuning can be accomplished by adjusting the shock absorber, most often while still on the car. In any case, changing the valving of shocks overall, in bump only or in rebound only, can change the handling of the car and improve lap times. For the most part, tuning with shocks is considered a fine-tuning adjustment, once the chassis is set up and tuned.

BOTTOMING OUT

If a shock bottoms or reaches full extension under load, handling can change dramatically and damage to the shock can occur. Often, the shock rod is bent and the internal piston is damaged. Bump stops on the shaft of the shocks reduce this and some chassis builders use rebound travel limiters to keep the shock from reaching full extension. Full extension is usually less of a problem.

COOLING

Shocks dampen by using friction, which causes heat. In technical terms, kinetic energy (motion) is turned into thermal energy (heat). Heat buildup can affect the rate of the shock, causing it to fade or lose damping capacity. Dissipating heat always helps shock performance. Bumpy tracks create more heat than smooth tracks. It is best not to cover shocks, and even to duct cool air to them. Aluminum shocks dissipate heat faster than steel bodies. For coil-overs, threaded body shocks cool better than smooth body shocks with thread spring perches over the body for the coil-over adjusters.

Shock absorbers, or more accurately suspension dampers, need to be correctly valved for each track. The width and diameter of the compression and rebound shim stacks determine the valving. These shim stacks can be changed to produce ideal handling and ride characteristics.

SHOCK TUNING

In the following example, a change in shock setup can provide an improvement. In the middle of a race, you are running just behind the race leader. He is pulling away slightly, and the place on the race track where he seems to gain is going into the corners under braking. You're driving in just as deep as you can, but the leader is able to drive in a half car length deeper. If you go in that hard, you pick up a small push. The car is great everywhere else, and you can run with the leader. Your cars are identical and on the same tires, so where could his advantage be? Even though you finish second, it's a frustrating race because you just can't quite run with the leader. The setup of the shock absorber may be the key to improving handling and picking up the pace

Shock setups don't cure problems. Shocks will not cure a big handling problem, though they can cause handling problems if they are bent, if they bind, or if they are way too stiff or soft. However, they can be great for making small improvement in handling in specific parts of the track or in a corner. In addition, shocks can be used to fine-tune the handling balance of a race car during transitions. In 95 percent of all cases, the baseline shocks, the ones recommended by your chassis builder for the type of track you're running, should be fine for the particular track you are racing. Extremely bumpy tracks may require a change to softer shocks if the car skates over the bumps or feels unstable. Many racers make the mistake of going too far away from the baseline setup and end up with an unworkable setup on the car.

Here are some important criteria for tuning with shocks, which could help make your car faster. Each tire contact patch *must* be optimized. Camber, caster, tire pressure, and toe must be correctly set up before tuning with shocks. If these suspension components aren't correctly set up, you're wasting time. Static weights and cross-weight percentages must be very close to optimum. The amount of stagger must be right. You need to make sure that the suspension components are not binding through the arc of travel. In addition, you need to determine where the problem occurs. Often, a driver does not recognize that a corner exit problem is a corner entry problem. A driver can easily overcompensate for a corner entry push, causing a loose condition on the exit. The handling

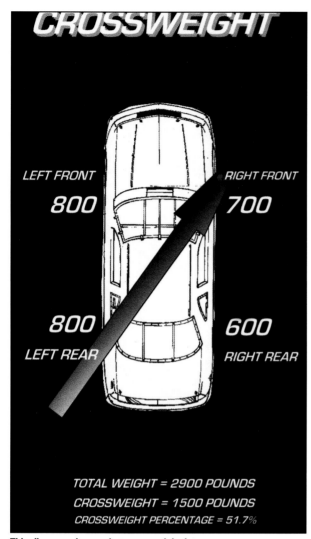

CROSSWEIGHT

LEFT FRONT

800

RIGHT FRONT

700

800

LEFT REAR

600

RIGHT REAR

TOTAL WEIGHT = 2900 POUNDS
CROSSWEIGHT = 1500 POUNDS
CROSSWEIGHT PERCENTAGE = 51.7%

This diagram shows what crossweight is.

pect too much. Get a good basic setup on your car, and small shock changes can pay big dividends.

HOW CROSSWEIGHT AFFECTS HANDLING

The correct technical term is crossweight percentage, but wedge or bite are the same thing. Crossweight is a great way to tune the chassis at the track, since it is easy to change, but even before a race car leaves the shop, setting weight percentages is critical.

STATIC WEIGHT DISTRIBUTION

One of the most important aspects of race car setup is the static weight distribution. With the car at rest and carrying the race setup, static weight distribution is the weight resting on each tire contact patch. This means the driver should be in the car, all fluids topped up and the fuel load should be consistent, usually a half-full tank. The car should be at minimum weight, using ballast as needed to make the proper weight.

When working with static weight distribution, we use two percentages to analyze the car's corner weights. Left-side weight percent and rear weight percent tell us all we need to know about the setup relative to the weight distribution. The left-side weight percentage is found by adding the left front weight to the left rear weight and dividing the sum by the total weight. The rear weight percentage is found in the same way. Add the left rear and the right rear weights together and divide the sum by the total weight. Many electronic scales will perform the calculations automatically.

Often, these percentages are mandated by rules, primarily for safety reasons and to keep racing costs down. The highest possible left-side weight percentage is the ideal target. Weight transfers from the inside of a vehicle to the outside when cornering. If more weight is on the left side to start, more weight will be placed on the left side in a left-hand turn. Since tire traction is proportional to the weight on a tire, the ideal situation is have equal weight on the left- and right-side tires in the middle of a corner. This means all four tires would be making the maximum amount of traction for that vehicle. In addition, tire traction would be at its highest and tire temperatures, as well as wear, would be equal between left and right. For this to occur, the static left-side weight would need to be between 58 percent and 59 percent. This is a

problem must be small. If it isn't, a larger problem in the setup must be solved. The car should already be fast. Don't expect more than .05 to .10 second improvement in lap times.

It takes a skilled, consistent driver who is sensitive to changes, to tune with shocks. New drivers should spend a test day making shock changes to the car to experience changes in the setup. This experience is extremely important to wring the last little bit of performance out of the car. A driver should make small changes. Going up or down two numbers or two clicks on adjustable shocks is a big change. And you should only change one corner at a time when tuning with shocks. Shocks are clearly a very valuable tuning tool on a stock car. Understanding what a shock can do is important. Getting the desired results takes effort and skill. Don't ex-

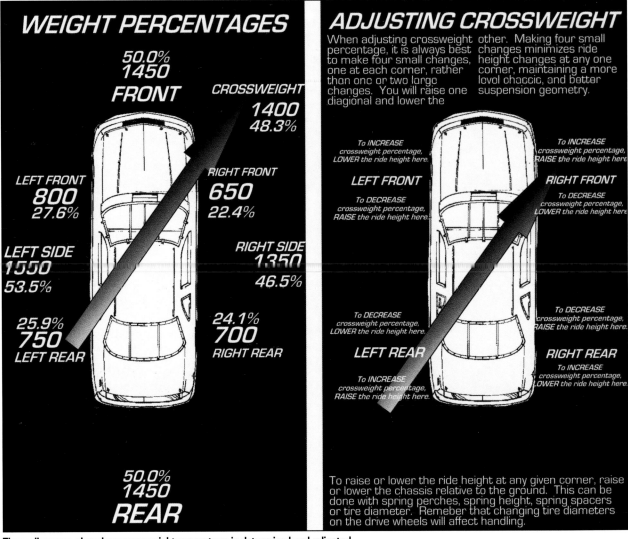

These diagrams show how crossweight percentage is determined and adjusted.

high percentage, and is almost always limited due to safety concerns. If a car gets crossed up to the right or has to turn right to avoid a crash, the possibility of the car rolling over, or at least spinning, increases. Additionally, racers would go to extremes if the left-side weight were not limited.

The same applies to rear weight percentage. Higher rear percentages would allow the car to accelerate off the turns better, but engine and driver location make weight percentages over 52 percent rear nearly impossible to obtain. Additionally, it is much more difficult to significantly change rear percentage because rear weight is mostly a design function. The only way to change the static weight distribution percentages is to physically move weight around in the car. Jacking weight will not alter the left-side or the rear percentages.

Fuel cell location, battery location, other major components and lead ballast all can be moved around to attain desired weight percentages.

CROSSWEIGHT PERCENTAGE

Racers have used crossweight percent for about 30 years, and today, electronic scales are commonplace, allowing accurate measurements in the shop or at the race track. The electronic scales perform the calculations and even store the data for future reference. But before the use of scales and crossweights, racers still had reliable ways to measure the same effects.

In the 1950s, maybe even before, racers used the phrase "wedge," which is still used today. It was called "wedge" because wooden wedges were hammered into the springs to change the ride height. Since most cars had leaf springs in the rear, the wedges were placed in the right front coil spring. This tightened the car up to compensate for tire stagger at the rear. The bigger the wedge, the greater the effect.

By the 1960s, weight jack screws were being used to change ride heights. This allowed faster, much more accurate tuning adjustments, so racers found a more accurate measurement. While still called wedge, wedges were not used. Wedge was measured by putting the rear axle housing on a jack and balanced on a socket (like the ones you use to change spark plugs). A sheet of paper was placed under the left rear tire and the jack raised until the paper could just be pulled out from under the left tire. If the rear tire was off the ground, wedge was present. If the left rear lifted first, there was reverse wedge. The wedge measurement was the distance between the tire and the ground. This was a good measurement, but not nearly as accurate or reliable as crossweight.

When race cars were first being weighed by racers on individual wheel scales (we used four grain scales in the early 1970s), racers noticed that the left rear weighed more when more wedge was present. The amount of difference in left rear versus right rear weight was called bite. More left rear weight meant more bite. The next step was looking at all four corners of the car and using what has become crossweight percentage.

Crossweight percentage compares the diagonal weight totals to the total car weight. To calculate crossweight percentage, add the right front weight to the left rear weight and divide the sum by the total weight of the car. Crossweight is also called wedge. If the percentage is over 50 percent, the car has wedge; below 50 percent the car has reverse wedge. More wedge means that the car will likely understeer more in a left turn. The advantage to wedge is that the left rear tire carries more load, so the car drives off the turns better. But in a right turn, the opposite occurs and the handling is worse. In almost all cases, the loss of cornering performance in one direction is greater than the gain in the other direction.

Crossweight is usually used in conjunction with tire stagger to balance handling. Stagger is the difference in circumference of the left rear tire compared to the right rear tire. Stagger is present when the right-side tire is bigger around. More stagger usually loosens the handling, so more crossweight is used to tighten the car up. This works really well on bias-ply tires with as much as 2 inches of circumference difference available. This is not the case with radial-ply tires. Radial tires are so uniform in their construction that very little stagger is possible, usually less than 1/2-an inch in circumference. In some instances, crossweight percentages under 50 percent are used with radial tires.

Understanding crossweight is crucial to a driver understanding race car dynamics. To truly understand crossweight and its affects, you need to understand how other systems affect handling. A driver should spend a test day and try different settings to evaluate what they do to the car. Make sure you use small changes and then work up to speed slowly until you have a feel and sense of what the changes will do.

SEVENTEEN

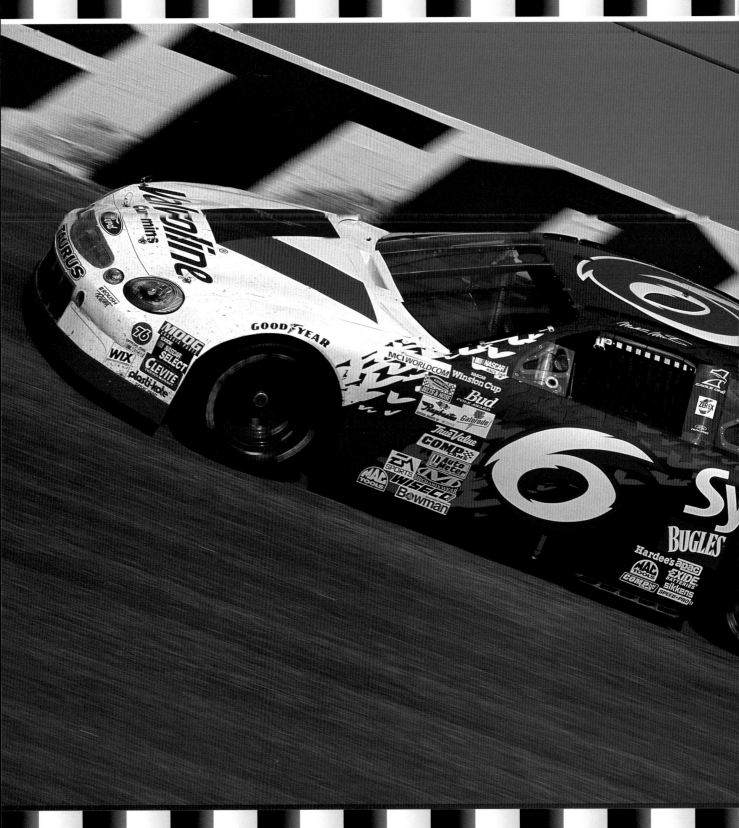

Aerodynamics for the Driver

D rag is the enemy of the race driver. Tire drag in the turns, drag under acceleration, and aerodynamic drag all reduce speed. One of the biggest factors is aero-drag, and not just on speedways. Aero-drag affects speed and acceleration even at very low track speeds. Many racers only look at aerodynamic drag and downforce where speeds exceed 100 miles per hour, but in reality, drag affects performance at all speeds. The effect is much greater at high speed, but gaining even 1/4 mile per hour at 70 miles per hour at the end of straight is vitally important. It can mean the difference between making a pass for position or being stuck behind the car in front. It may take five extra horsepower to find that 1/4 mile per hour, or a reduction in aero-drag. Of course, the team that gains an advantage in both horsepower and aerodynamics is going to very competitive.

To move a stock car through the air at 195 miles per hour requires about 450 horsepower. NASCAR restrictor plate engines produce this amount of horsepower. To go faster takes more horsepower or less drag. At 195 miles per hour, the drag on a stock car equals the horsepower output. In order to improve performance, the ratio of power to drag must be changed, which means more power or less drag. To increase speed by 5 miles per hour requires about 50 more horsepower, which is not any easy task with the restrictor plate. On the other side of the scale, a three percent reduction in drag results in the same speed gain. While no easier than finding horsepower, drag reduction does offer an alternative to the horsepower

Mark Martin and other top drivers manage their tires because a race can be won or lost depending on tire health. If a driver drives too hard and wears out the tires before a scheduled pit stop or at a critical part of the race, he or she will lose track position. *Nigel Kinrade*

quest. And it also points out the huge importance of aerodynamics on a superspeedway.

But the superspeedway isn't the only place where aerodynamics play a role, and drag is not the only consideration. Downforce increases traction for braking, cornering, and acceleration off the corners. Increasing downforce is an important part of aerodynamic engineering. The trick is finding the best balance between drag reduction and downforce. Since these two factors are not compatible, finding the best compromise is necessary for a race team to run competitively, let alone gain an advantage.

AERODYNAMIC FACTORS

When looking at aerodynamics relative to on-track performance, two factors are considered. Drag, or the force caused by wind resistance, slows the car. Downforce, or negative lift, affects tire traction. First, let's look at drag.

The easiest way to experience aerodynamic drag is to put your hand out the window of a car moving at 60 miles per hour. Hold you palm for-

ward and feel the wind pressure pushing your hand back. At 60 miles per hour, the wind force makes it difficult to hold your hand steady. It takes considerable muscle strength to hold your hand stationary relative to your car.

The force against your hand is aerodynamic drag. The force against your hand is proportional to the area of your hand. If you put on a glove that makes your hand twice as big, the force against your hand will double. Rotate your hand so that the area at a right angle to the direction of air flow is one-half the size of your hand, and the force against your hand is cut in half.

Obviously, reducing frontal area as much as possible reduces aerodynamic drag and improves performance on the track. On a stock car, the frontal area is most often specified by racing associations based on body templates. Each body must match the spec bodies. The typical frontal area on a stock car is just under 20 square feet.

The speed of the car moving through the air determines the amount of aerodynamic drag. This

In Winston Cup racing, aerodynamic efficiency is crucial for success. In short oval racing, aerodynamics are not as important, but are still a relevant consideration. This photo provides a good perspective of the front fascia and air dam on the 2000 Chevy Monte Carlo driven by Bobby Hamilton, and the 2000 Pontiac Grand Prix driven by Tony Stewart. *Paul Johnson/Speed Sports Photography*

is a much bigger factor, however. If you double the speed, the aerodynamic drag force is four times greater. Put your hand back out the window at 60 miles per hour. Let's say the force pushing against your hand is 25 pounds at that speed. If we double the speed to 120 miles per hour, the force will quadruple to 100 pounds pushing against your hand. If we cut the speed to 30 miles per hour, the force is reduced to 6.25 pounds.

One way to reduce aerodynamic drag on a race car is to slow down, not a very good option. It takes about 115 horsepower to overcome aerodynamic drag on a stock car at 100 miles per hour. To go 200 miles per hour requires an increase of four times the horsepower, or about 460 horsepower. That's about the power a restrictor plate engine produces. Without a restrictor plate, a stock car would have a top speed of about 250 miles per hour, which would mean a lap speed at Daytona of around 220 to 225 miles per hour.

Finally, body shape affects aerodynamic drag forces. If your rotate your hand so that your palm is facing the ground, you are reducing frontal area, but you also change the shape of your hand. The more "slippery" shape also reduces drag. A given shape of an object will have a specific effect on air flow over that shape. This is called the drag coefficient. The drag coefficient times the frontal area gives the relative amount of aerodynamic drag at a given speed. A larger drag coefficient means more aerodynamic drag. Most of the work done by race teams and auto manufacturers focuses on reducing aerodynamic drag coefficients.

A flat plate headed directly into the air stream has a drag coefficient of almost 1.2. A smooth ball has a drag coefficient of 0.47. A streamlined body, such as a symmetrical airplane wing, has a drag coefficient of 0.04, about as low as possible. Given equal frontal area, if your open hand against the wind flow created 25 pounds of drag force, then the streamlined shape of the same frontal

area would create only 1 pound of force. That's a huge difference.

Interestingly, if we take that streamlined shape, cut it in half and put it on the ground, the drag coefficient more than doubles to 0.09. The ground has a big effect on drag, always increasing it. Pilots know about this effect, called the ground effect, when landing a plane. Rotating wheels also increase the drag coefficient. With significant effort, the drag coefficient on a stock car has been lowered to about 0.28 to 0.29, a fairly small number, and lower than the drag coefficient on an Indy car or Formula 1 car. While a major factor on speedways, aerodynamics has a considerable affect even a 1/2 mile oval.

KEY AREAS OF AERODYNAMIC PERFORMANCE

Two key factors affect car performance aerodynamically. Drag reduces top speed for a given horsepower and also reduces acceleration. Total downforce or lift affects traction. Any positive lift reduces traction. Downforce, or negative lift, increases the load on the tires and therefore increases traction. More downforce means more traction, and that is desirable in most situations. But downforce is expensive in terms of aerodynamic drag. More downforce means more drag. The ideal compromise is key. The better the compromise, the better the on-track performance. The compromise is called the lift/drag ratio. How much lift (or downforce) is present for a given amount of drag. This can be measured in a wind tunnel or during testing.

Several things can cause the flow to become disrupted and increase drag:

- **Seams between body panels**
- **Window openings**
- **The shape of the body panels themselves**
- **Ripples in body panels**
- **Duct openings**
- **Abrupt changes in the angles of body panels**

> **The closer you get to the car in front of you when drafting, the more air it takes off the rear spoiler, and that causes the car ahead to get loose.**
>
> *–Jeff Gordon*

> **It's hard to fix aerodynamic problems. Sometimes you think it's a chassis thing, but it's really an aero problem. It's hard to overcome the aero problem.**
>
> *–Jeff Burton*

Bill Elliott flies his No. 94 McDonald's Thunderbird at Charlotte Motor Speedway (now called Lowe's Motor Speedway). At Charlotte, like other many other ovals, aerodynamic s play a big role in potential success. A driver is constantly searching for a balanced setup with adequate downforce and the lowest drag. *Nigel Kinrade*

Sometimes adding a bump or small ripple in an area on the body can improve flow in a trouble spot but create a small amount of turbulence ahead of the problem. These are called vortex generators, and they often reduce overall drag by increasing drag a little bit in one place to reduce it more elsewhere.

After the coefficient of drag has been minimized for the body shape, internal air flow must be checked through radiator openings, brake ducts, air intakes and driver cooling. A balance must be struck between the needs of the various systems of the car. If drag is reduced, but air flow to the radiator is also reduced and the car overheats, the benefits are not worth the price. Cooling the brakes on short tracks is critical, and getting air to the driver is very important for those long events. And once the air enters the bodywork to perform a task, the air must also exit the car in a way that minimize

the negative effects of drag and lift. And great care is taken by many teams to assure that internal aerodynamics are addressed. If flow can be handled more efficiently inside the bodywork of the car for cooling and engine intake air, then smaller, more efficient openings can be used, further reducing overall drag. The needs of the various race car systems are often not complementary, and much time and money goes into finding the most effective compromises.

TUNING AERODYNAMICS AT THE TRACK

Let's look at the factors a team must consider when seeking the best compromise between aerodynamic drag and downforce, as well as overall system performance. There are several ways a race team can accomplish this.

- **Rear spoiler angle**
- **Radiator opening**

- **Brake ducting**
- **Rear quarter panel profile**
- **Air dam profile in front of the front fender wells**
- **Air dam height**
- **Window openings**
- **Chassis setup**

> The chassis balance is much more important on a short track than aerodynamic balance. On tracks 1 mile or longer, the aero becomes more important.
>
> *–Terry Labonte*

The hardest part of the crew's job is to determine priorities for each track and race situation. For example, brake ducting is virtually unnecessary at the Daytona and Talladega superspeedways. The brakes are only used entering the pits or to avoid a crash, so heat buildup is minimal. But at a track like Martinsville, the demands on brakes are extreme. The brakes are applied once every nine seconds for about two seconds, slowing 3,600 pounds from 110 miles per hour to about 50 miles per hour. The kinetic energy converted to heat is enormous. Brake rotors glow red hot during each brake application. During a race, the brakes are applied like this about 1,000 times, with precious little time in-between applications for the brakes to cool. Thus, good brake cooling at Martinsville is far more important than total aerodynamic drag. But most tracks are in between, with varying requirements for cooling and aerodynamic efficiency. Open the ducts and intakes too much, and drag increases; keep them too small, and brake or engine overheating results. It's a moving target, like many systems on the race car, and the teams finding the best compromises are the most competitive.

The air intake for systems cooling and engine air is only half the picture. Downforce versus aerodynamic drag is the other part of the aerodynamic picture. Again the needs vary widely from track to track. Take Daytona. Top speed is critical for performance. Reduced drag is everything. Even the radiator intake is taped over during qualifying to minimize drag. Other tracks require as much downforce as possible. Any speedway a mile or less, the road courses, and short tracks all require maximum downforce. Even at 60 miles per hour, excessive aerodynamic drag can reduce performance. But within the range of optimal lift/drag ratios, the team can make changes that affect the amount of downforce versus drag. And this affects the handling balance of the race car, especially at high speed.

The most obvious and common downforce adjustment is the rear spoiler angle. Racing associations dictate the size and shape of the spoiler, and a minimum angle. Beyond that the angle is an adjustment that can be made easily, even during a pit stop. Increasing the angle of attack increases downforce as well as drag. The downforce adds traction to the rear tires, so that handling balance is affected. More downforce at the rear will tighten a loose handling condition. There is a limit to the spoiler angle, however. Increase the angle too much, and the spoiler will stall, just like a wing on an airplane. When the spoiler begins to stall, drag goes way up and downforce is lost almost completely. A stalled spoiler is not a good thing on a race car. Finding the sweet spot is always the goal.

In addition to the spoiler, the rear quarter panels can be moved in and out relative to the tire to affect flow under the car and coming off the rear tires. This changes downforce slightly, and is an easy way to affect handling balance. At the front, the air dam just in front of the front wheels can also be moved in and out to change air flow under the car and around the tires, affecting front downforce. The air dam height above the ground can be altered slightly to change downforce. The ground clearance, however, is limited by rules, making this less desirable as a tuning tool. Raising the air dam too high not only creates considerable drag but also creates lift, hurting tire traction at the front.

In summary, aerodynamics plays a major role in performance on the race track. Finding the optimum setting to make the best use of air flow by minimizing drag, optimizing cooling needs, and increasing downforce is one of many challenges facing every team each time it hits the race track. The team finding the best balance between all of the factors affecting performance stands the best chance of starting the race from the pole. Then the challenge begins all over again, as the teams search for the best balance for the different needs of racing with other cars on the track.

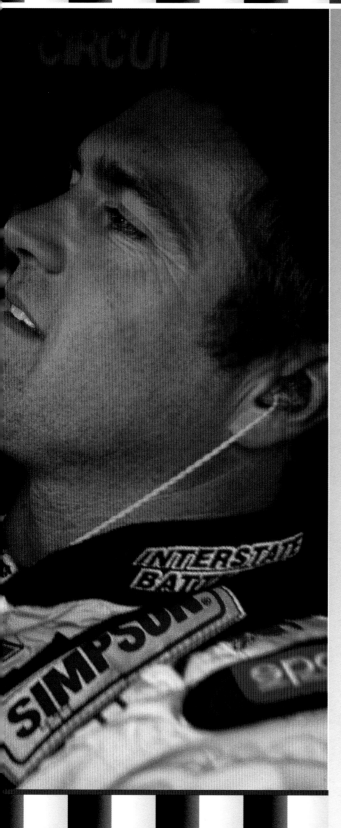

EIGHTEEN

Safety Equipment for the Race Driver

Racing is dangerous. Serious injuries, even fatal ones are possible. Who would have ever thought that Dale Earnhardt could die in a crash? The best possible safety equipment reduces the risk. A driver needs to use it and care for it properly if you value your well-being.

There are certain realities of racing. First, racing is dangerous. The best safety equipment reduces risk, but of course, does not eliminate it. Drivers needs to diligently maintain safety equipment. Safety should never be compromised. If seat belts are worn or frayed, replace them. If a helmet has sustained an impact, buy a new one.

Even the most safety-conscious racing associations like SCCA (Sports Car Club of America), FIA (Federation Internationale de l'Automobile) and NHRA (National Hot Rod Association) cannot be on top of every detail every minute. And considering that most stock car racing associations are less stringent about safety rules, especially rules relating to a driver's personal gear, the onus of safety falls to the driver. After all, it's your neck on the line.

A driver should never cut corners when it comes to safety. One should never buy or use old, worn, or second rate helmets, belts, or racing seats. Ultimately, the driver must realize that it's his or her own neck on the line. Like other Winston Cup drivers, Bobby Labonte uses the best safety equipment the market has to offer. Likewise, a grass roots racer should use the best available equipment. *Nigel Kinrade*

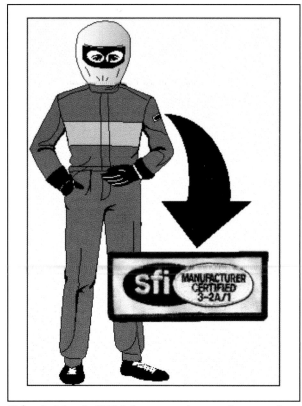

Always look for the SFI label to assure that your fire protection meets the stringent standards of the SFI Foundation. Courtesy *SFI Foundation*

Product Certification

Several groups test motorsports safety equipment to ensure that it offers the greatest protection to drivers. The testing is rigorous and the standards are demanding. In some cases, products are date-certified to assure that drivers are protected from product deterioration. For products with a testing standard, it would be foolish for a driver to use products that do not meet the specs of one of the testing groups.

SFI Foundation

SFI is a nonprofit organization established to issue and administer standards for all kinds of specialty and performance automotive and racing equipment. Manufacturers of equipment are the primary users of SFI standards. Some sanctioning bodies have adopted some standards for their rules. Ultimately, the consumer benefits from the program because it establishes recognized levels of performance or standards of quality for a product, such as driver restraint assemblies. You can be certain that products with an SFI Foundation tag or sticker provide the best possible protection.

A good driver restraint system is one of the most important items for protecting the driver in a crash.

Snell Memorial Foundation

Snell tests only helmets. Any helmet used for auto racing should have the Snell SA 95 or SA 2000 rating, or the SFI 31 or 31.2 sticker.

FIA

The FIA is an international sanctioning body that specifies stringent safety regulations for auto racing. Any FIA-approved product assures that you have the best possible protection. FIA uses the SFI Foundation and Snell-approved tests on applicable products.

DRIVER RESTRAINT SYSTEM

An integral part of safety equipment is the driver restraint assembly, or seat belts, to keep the driver inside the roll cage where the least amount of injury will occur in a crash. A restraint assembly consists of several components, each with a specific function. The shoulder harness provides one strap for each shoulder and is intended to restrain movement of the upper torso and shoulder regions. An optional cross strap across the chest can be used to hold the shoulder harness together. The lap belt restrains movement of the pelvis and the antisubmarine strap prevents the pelvis from slipping forward from under the lap belt in the event of an accident.

The purchase of belts should be based on more important criteria than whether or not the color matches the car. A driver should look at the performance specifications of one manufacturer's restraint assembly in comparison to others. Manufacturers whose products pass the standard laboratory tests participate in the SFI Foundation's certification program.

The standard that applies to safety belts is SFI Specification 16.1. The spec defines a driver restraint assembly and outlines basic design dimensions and requirements. It also describes the testing procedures in detail and explains how to interpret the test results to determine if the product meets the required criteria and thus passes the test.

Once a product is passed, the manufacturer installs SFI certification tags on the belts, which display the date of manufacture. Dated certification tags enable drivers and race officials to easily determine the age of the belts. One of the most important requirements of the specification states that the useful life of the webbing in the straps of the restraint assembly shall not exceed two years, and they must be replaced at or before that time. Only the original manufacturer can reweb an assembly prior to recertifying. Driver restraints should be inspected and recertified every two years.

Restraints must be maintained, inspected, and

> **Something we do about every other lap is check our belts and make sure they don't work loose.**
>
> *–Ricky Rudd*

> **Shoulder harnesses can loosen up during a race, not a lot but a little, so you check them and pull them tight, usually during a caution or pit stop.**
>
> *–Terry Labonte*

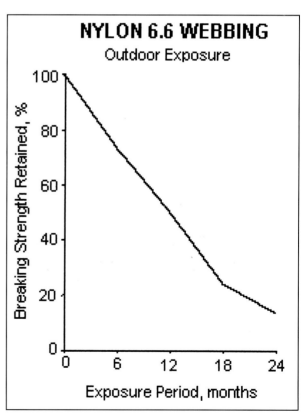

This graph depicts the deterioration of nylon restraint system webbing over time due to outdoor exposure. Webbing should be replaced at least every two years to assure maximum protection in a crash. **Courtesy *SFI Foundation***

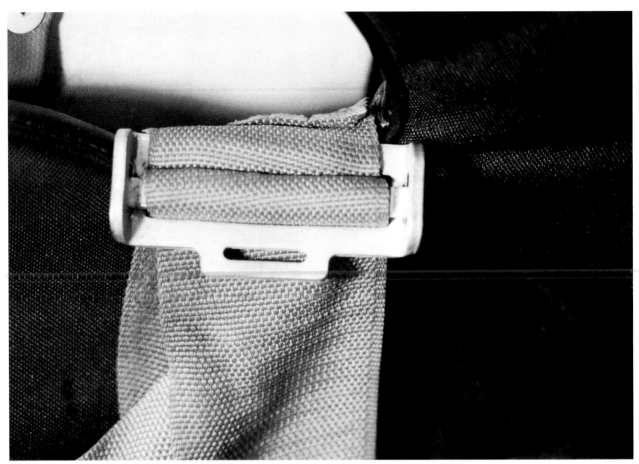

Check the harness and lap belt adjusters to make sure they work smoothly and freely. Clean and inspect before every race event.

replaced or rewebbed every two years because they degenerate from exposure to the elements and over time. Prolonged exposure of seat belt webbing and thread to sunlight can cause degradation of the fibers and loss of restraint integrity. The rate at which the breaking strength of the webbing decreases with outdoor exposure is illustrated in the graph below. The webbing used in motorsports restraints is typically made with DuPont Nylon 6-6 or a similar product. According to the data, the webbing loses about half of its strength in one year.

With this kind of rapid deterioration, it is obvious why replacing the webbing every two years is essential to driver safety. Old and weakened belts could easily snap under the loads imposed upon them in an accident situation. Failure to properly restrain the driver in a crash would have devastating consequences.

The effectiveness of a restraint assembly is also influenced by attachment techniques. The principal precaution for installing the mounting hardware to the vehicle is to minimize bending stress in the fitting. This is achieved by making sure the belts pull from a straight angle against the hardware. The assembly should be installed so the straps do not rub against any surface that can cause the webbing to fray. The anchoring mechanisms should also periodically be checked so that they don't become loose or weakened. Proper installation of the restraint assembly also means achieving the correct fit to the driver. Belts should be as short as possible to reduce stretching and better restraint of driver movement.

The attachment points must provide the optimum geometry to minimize movement of the belts. Lap belts perform best when they act at an angle between 45 and 55 degrees relative to the longitudinal axis of the vehicle as illustrated in Part A of the figure. This angle permits the lap belt to react to the upward pull of the shoulder harness. A system installed with a shallow belt angle, as shown in Part B of the figure, permits the shoulder harness to pull the lap belt up off the pelvic area and into the abdominal region, with the likelihood of injury to internal organs.

The end attachments of the shoulder harness must also be installed at appropriate angles. The ideal position is anywhere between 5 degrees below and 30 degrees above the driver's shoulder. If the upper attachment point falls significantly below the driver's shoulder, a spinal compression injury is likely to occur. In an accident situation, the shoulder belts pull down and back on the torso as they resist the forward motion of the driver. The resultant restraint force compresses the spinal column. In addition, the force of the crash impact will add to the stresses on the spine.

On the other hand, if the trailing ends of the harness are too far above the shoulder (greater than 30 degrees), then two problems can occur. First, tension in the shoulder harness is increased and undue stress is applied to the harness and its structural attachments. Second, excessive angle will cause excessive motion. If the harness belts are too far above the shoulder, they will provide little resistance to forward motion of the driver's upper torso. The result is impact with the steering wheel and the possibility of neck injury. The shoulder straps should also be 3 to 6 inches apart behind the driver's neck to prevent slipping off of the shoulders.

The reliability of a restraint system is greatly affected by the way it is installed. It is imperative to follow the installation instructions provided by the seat belt manufacturer. Also, the necessity of replacing or rewebbing seat belts every two years cannot be overstressed.

DRIVER SUITS

No matter how much you already know, or don't know, about driver suits, the SFI Foundation Specification 3.2A is a standard that will guide you in your choice of a well-made garment. You have probably noticed the black and white SFI patch on many drivers' left shoulders at various tracks. The patch demonstrates that the manufacturer certifies the suit to meet or exceed the SFI specification.

What does this mean to the consumer? It means that there is a way to differentiate the quality-assured products from the untested products. A driver suit, certified to meet the SFI spec has been laboratory tested and has passed the requirements of that test. Before getting into the details of the

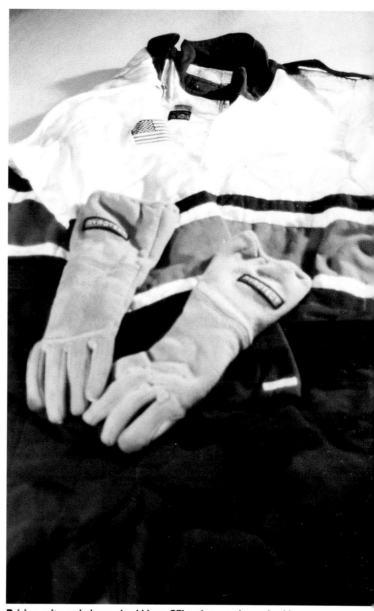

Driving suits and gloves should have SFI ratings, and you should always use multi-layer suits and gloves with Nomex or other approved underwear.

testing procedures, it is necessary to understand what the SFI Foundation is and what it does.

The driver suit spec 3.2A tests a garment's fire-retardant capabilities. The spec contains a rating system based on the garment's capability to provide Thermal Protective Performance (TPP) in the presence of both direct flame and radiant heat. The purpose of the TPP is to measure the length of time the person wearing the garment can be exposed to a heat source before incurring a second degree, or skin-blistering burn.

The TPP rating is the product of exposure heat flux and exposure time. The TPP results can be converted to the length of time before a second-degree burn occurs. The higher the garment rating, the more protection the suit offers before a second-degree burn occurs. Here are the SFI ratings with the corresponding TPP values and times to a second-degree burn.

Another test included in the chart is the after-flame test. When a direct flame is applied to the fabric and then removed, the time it takes the material to self-extinguish is measured. This is called after-flame time, and it must be two seconds or less for the layer of fabric to pass. Cuff material is also subjected to this test.

The flammability test evaluates single layers of fabric only. The individual layers of a multiple-layer suit are tested for after-flame time separately.

The TPP test can be used to evaluate multiple-layer configurations as well as single-layer fabrics. The samples used in testing are assembled with the identical fabrics and layer order as an actual driver suit.

Other tests required by Spec 3.2A include thread heat resistance, zipper heat resistance, and multiple layer thermal shrinkage resistance. A common misunderstanding about SFI ratings is that they represent the number of fabric layers in the garment. It is actually possible for driver suits with various numbers of layers to have the same performance rating. This is due to the wide range of materials used by manufacturers today.

The radiant heat portion of the spec is very important because the majority of racer burns are caused by heat transfer rather than direct flame. Insulation is the best way to prevent this kind of burn. Using multiple layers of fabric helps keep the heat source away from the skin longer because each layer creates air gaps that have to heat up. The extra seconds gained with each layer are precious to a driver trying to escape from a burning car.

Racing underwear provides additional protection. Nomex underwear should be worn with every type of driver suit, especially single-layer suits, because it will double the protection time (plus three seconds). The 3.2A rating does not include underwear. It is certified through SFI Spec 3.3 for Driver Accessories and undergoes the same TPP and flammability tests as the driver suit outerwear.

A garment's insulation capability is also affected by the fit of the suit. A suit worn too tight will compress the air gaps and allow heat to reach the skin faster.

There are other things you can do besides finding a correct fit to optimize the protection performance of your driver suit. Ideally, you want to wash your suit after every event. Most suits are machine washable, but manufacturers usually recommend dry cleaning. It is absolutely essential to read the care tag on the garment and closely follow the manufacturer's instructions.

You should avoid wearing your suit while working on the car. Not only would you be ruining an expensive piece of equipment, but you would essentially be inviting a fire to burn you. Grease, fuel, oil, and even cleaning fluids can soak into the fabric and support the flames of a fire, causing high heat. Fluids soaked into a suit also produce steam when exposed to heat and cause liquid vaporization burns.

Part of maintaining safety equipment effectively is taking good care of your driving gear. Any piece of fire retardant clothing needs to be clean in order to provide effective fire protection. Grease and oil on a driving suit, gloves or shoes is like adding fuel to a fire. I personally do not want to wear the makings of a torch when I drive a race car. Wash your driving suit and gloves per manufacturer's instructions. This really should be done after every event or once a week if you run more than once every seven days. Make sure shoes and neck braces are clean.

If you are ever involved in a fire, discard your suit and get a new one. Even the smallest singe produces weak spot in the material and that weak spot can fail if exposed to fire again. Proper maintenance of a driver suit will help extend its useful life and provide you with years of protection.

HELMETS

Helmets are composed of different components, and each has its own purpose. The hard outer shell provides the primary defense against impact. It is filled with Energy Absorbing Material (EAM), sometimes called the liner, that absorbs impact energy and reduces trauma to the head. The helmet's padding is sometimes confused with the liner. Unlike the liner, the padding does not absorb energy. The padding is intended for sizing and comfort

A helmet with the Snell 95, Snell 2000, or SFI Foundation sticker is a must. Do not use old helmets or motorcycle helmets. Auto racing helmets have liners designed to absorb impact from roll cage tubes, and the helmet lining is made from fire-retardant material to reduce the risk of facial burns in a fire.

only. The padding and EAM are covered by a fire retardant lining. This lining is the only part of the helmet that comes in contact with the wearer's head. On full face helmets, the clear shield provides facial protection while allowing the driver to see the track ahead. Then there is the retention system, which is made up of the straps and hardware that secure the helmet to the driver's head.

Most manufacturers construct these components with state-of-the-art composite materials, such as Kevlar or carbon fiber, that make the helmets light and comfortable to wear. Of course, the intended function of the helmet is much more important than

a comfortable fit. Reputable manufacturers ensure that their helmets provide the necessary protection in a crash by submitting samples of their products for performance testing and by participating in a quality assurance certification program.

There are two levels of SFI specifications that pertain to helmets, competition, and motorsports. The competition specifications are designated SFI Spec 31.1 Open Face Helmets and SFI Spec 31.2 Full Face Helmets. The motorsports helmet specs are numbered 41.1 and 41.2 for open and full face helmets, respectively. Snell uses similar specifications and standards for testing.

The two levels of helmet specifications require the same criteria for impact protection. The difference between the two classifications is that specs 31.1 and 31.2 require fire-resistance testing, and specs 41.1 and 41.2 do not. Helmets tested to the motorsports specifications (41.1 and 41.2) are primarily used in motorcycle applications. Some sanctioning bodies may permit the use of these helmets in various auto racing classes. However, do not use SFI 41.1 and 41.2 or Snell M rated helmets for stock car racing. Serious burns can result. Use only helmets with a fire-retardant lining. And it's a really good idea to use only full face helmets in stock cars. They offer much greater protection in a crash.

Helmets tested to the SFI specs are required to resist the elements that they would be exposed to in normal use. They include low temperature, high temperature, and moisture. Besides environmental considerations, helmets must resist fluids used in and around motor vehicles. Helmets exposed to these environments are then subjected to a series of impact attenuation tests. Impact attenuation is the ability of a helmet to absorb the energy of an impact, thus reducing the force to the wearer's head. In these tests, helmets are fitted on metal headforms and the helmet/headform assemblies are dropped on several steel anvils of various shapes. The anvils simulate different surfaces that a helmet could come in contact with during a crash. The impacts are guided free falls, dropped from controlled heights on a testing apparatus.

The headform is equipped with a transducer to record peak acceleration, measured in gs. Peak acceleration is the amount of energy transferred to the test headform when it impacts the test surface. For a helmet to pass, the headform must receive no more than 300 gs of energy for any given drop. Additionally, the peak acceleration for the average of all drops for a single helmet may not exceed 275 gs.

Since the purpose of a helmet is to protect a racer from both impact and fire, the SFI competition specs include flame-resistance tests. A 790-degree Celsius propane flame is applied to the shell, trim, chin strap, and face shield (on a full face helmet). The exact time that the flame is applied to the samples varies depending on the component. For example, the required thermal load for the chin strap is 15 seconds, while the face shield is subjected to flame for 45 seconds.

Any flames that develop on the helmet components must self-extinguish and the time it takes for the flames to go out is measured. This is called after-flame time. The after-flame time must be less than a given time for each component if the helmet is to pass this portion of the spec. The lining is subjected to a radiant heat test in addition to the direct flame test. This is the same Thermal Protective Performance (TPP) test that is required in the SFI Specification 3.2A for driver suits. In fact, the helmet liner must meet the same criteria as a 3.2A/1 driver suit.

The face shield also undergoes a number of specialized tests in the SFI specifications for helmets. Optical properties are checked to ensure that the driver will have clear and undistorted vision. The fastening mechanism must keep the shield latched to the helmet in the event of an impact. Also, the shield must not allow penetration from either a dropped projectile or a steel ball that is fired at the shield during penetration testing.

Other tests required by the helmet specs are visual clearance of the facial opening, chin strap strength, and a chin bar impact test. The chin bar test is applicable only to full-face helmets. Racers need to know that their helmets that have undergone extensive and thorough testing, as described above.

The SFI Quality Assurance Program also requires the manufacturers to retest their helmets every two years. This ensures that their products meet the specification requirements on an ongoing basis. Manufacturers who participate in the SFI program and certify their helmets to the SFI specifications will display conformance labels on the inside of their helmets. The SFI label is proof to consumers that they are purchasing a quality-assured product that has been tested in a continuing effort to improve motorsports safety.

Helmets should be clean, but never use solvent to clean a helmet, as the poly plastics can be severely weakened. And be careful when having a helmet painted. Check with the helmet manufacturer about paint compatibility. A great looking paint job that weakens your helmet's outer shell is not a good thing.

SEAT

One of the most important pieces of driver safety equipment is the racing seat. For stock car racing,

A good aluminum racing seat offers added protection in a crash and provides an excellent feel for the race car. Make sure it fits snugly and is securely attached to the floor or cage members in at least four spots on the bottom and two places on the back support. Having the seat come lose in a crash is contrary to reducing injuries. Follow the seat manufacturer's installation and care instructions.

use an aluminum seat from one of the several reputable manufacturers. The seat should have a snug fit, and they come in a variety of sizes to accommodate different builds. Various attachments are available to provide head restraint and leg support.

A universal joint in the steering shaft is mandatory for driver protection in a frontal impact. Make sure the joints are clean and the bolts tight at least every four races.

SFI does not have a racing seat certification program as of this writing, so shop with care. Make sure the seat is rigid, and very securely bolted to the floor pan and the roll cage so that it cannot come loose in a crash. Use Grade 8 or aircraft quality mounting hardware of the specifications recommended by the seat manufacturer.

STEERING COMPONENTS

The steering system in your car should have both a collapsible steering column and U-joints to provide added protection in the event of a crash, especially with any kind of frontal impact. These components are not currently tested to a standard criteria, but companies like Borgeson and Sweet offer excellent products.

THE HANS DEVICE

As this book is being written, four NASCAR drivers have died in racing crashes. The cause of death in each case was from basal skull fractures, an injury caused by excessive forces acting on the neck and head, resulting in a bone fracture at the base of the skull. Three of the deaths were instant, and one driver died the next day. The fracture can cause trauma to the brain and may cause arteries to be severed in the neck, resulting in

Clean and lubricate the hex end of the quick-release steering system several times a season.

near instant, extreme blood loss. In each of the fatalities, the HANS (Head And Neck Support) Device would have greatly increased the chances of survival. The HANS Device restrains the head in a head-on or near head-on impact. The restraining system holds the head stationary relative to the body, keeping the head from the violent motions associated with a serious crash. This greatly reduces the chances of traumatic brain injuries and basal skull fractures.

The HANS Device was invented by Dr. Robert Hubbard, professor at the College of Engineering at Michigan State University, in collaboration with his brother-in-law, long-time IMSA sports car driver Jim Downing. The objective was to reduce the chance of serious injury caused by the violent movement of the unrestrained head and helmet combination.

The patented (4638510, 6009566) biomechanical design utilizes a collar and yoke system constructed of carbon fiber and Kevlar. The device is worn on the upper body under the shoulder straps. It is connected to the helmet by two or three flexible tethers that allow normal movement of the head (left, right, up, and down), but limit extreme head motions and neck loads. After a few laps wearing the HANS unit, most drivers forget they have it on.

After years of testing (sled crashes at Wayne State University and General Motors), and use under actual race conditions by Downing, the Model-I HANS was offered for sale in 1991. More than 300 are now in active use worldwide. There have been numerous reports of its effectiveness in real racing accidents.

In 1997, Hubbard/Downing, Inc. contracted with DaimlerBenz for joint testing and development of a HANS for Formula One. In April 2000, Daimler-Chrysler and the FIA made a joint announcement that they have found the HANS safety system the most effective method of head and neck protection currently available for drivers.

OTHER SAFETY EQUIPMENT

Additional safety equipment, whether required or not, includes the following:
- **Fuel cell**
- **Window net**
- **Fire suppression system**
- **Roll bar padding**
- **Steering wheel quick disconnect/release**
- **Driver accessories—underwear, gloves, shoes**

There is little in this cockpit that could cause injury. Some additional roll bar padding would reduce possible injuries even more.

Inspect the belt mounting tabs for wear and welds at least twice a season.

The driver needs to make sure that a cam lock quick release system on a driver restraint system operates smoothly, especially under load. If it does not, one should have it checked by the manufacturer.

The shoulder harnesses must pull from behind, not at the base of the seat. Make sure the belts pass over the bar as shown, or the shoulder harnesses will not properly restrain you in a crash.

It is important to use the best equipment you can obtain. All of these items have SFI certification, so look for SFI tags and stickers. These items can reduce injuries and save your life.

CARE AND MAINTENANCE OF COCKPIT SAFETY EQUIPMENT

None of us really want to think about what can happen to our bodies when we slam into a wall, or worse. But the reality is that crashes happen, and the more prepared we are the less likely that injuries will occur. And a big part of that preparation is taking good care of the safety equipment in the cockpit of your race car.

While the car owner has a responsibility to provide good, functional safety equipment for the driver,

it's the driver butt strapped into the seat, so the final responsibility when it comes to personal safety is the driver's. Several years ago I was invited to drive a limited late-model stock car in a local race. The car was less than well prepared, but what kept me from racing the car was the driver restraint. The material was so stiff from aging that it was hard to bend the lap belts. While my ability to visualize what can happen to me in a crash is way below average, this situation allowed me to vividly see what could happen if I crashed and those old belts came apart. That mental image made the decision not to drive that car easy. And after looking, the belts had been made about 15 years earlier. Since the driver restraint system is the most important part of the cockpit driver safety package, let's start there.

Driver Restraint System

The above story should never occur. The webbing on each component of the driver restraint system should be replaced at least every two seasons. The reason is simple. The elements like smog and heat deteriorate the webbing material with time. This weakens the material, reducing its tensile strength and its ability to stretch without ripping apart. The tensile strength combined with the ability to stretch under load is exactly what helps absorb the energy in a crash. It's obvious what can happen if the webbing breaks, but less obvious is the reduced ability over time of the material to stretch. Reduced stretch, even if failure does not occur, reduces the ability of the belts to absorb impact. More of the energy is passed along to the driver, and injuries are more likely and more severe when the driver takes more of the impact energy. Simply put, new webbing or new belts will reduce the severity of injuries in a crash. So if your restraint system is over two years old, the webbing needs to be replaced. It's inexpensive compared to new restraints and if it reduces injuries, it's priceless.

In between replacement cycles, simple maintenance will increase the life and function of your belts. Belts get dirty. Wash them with soap and water. If they get oil or grease on them, wash them immediately. Oil products deteriorate the webbing material. Also check the latch mechanism for function and dirt. Belts should be cleaned after every event. Do not use any type of flammable solvent for cleaning belt webbing.

Restraint System Mounting Hardware

Like webbing material, hardware corrodes. Replace the nuts and bolts when the webbing is replaced. Use only the hardware provided by the belt manufacturer and always use lock nuts on belt mounts. Never leave free play on a flush mount bracket and make sure eye bolts are tightened so the flange on the bolt is against the bracket and the eye bolt has no lateral free play. If you have the snap-in style belts, be sure to use a cotter pin in the provided hole to assure that the snap cannot open accidentally.

Brackets for belts should be aligned to minimize bending load on the bracket. Eye bolts should have the belt, when loaded, pull on a direct line passing through the shank of the bolt.

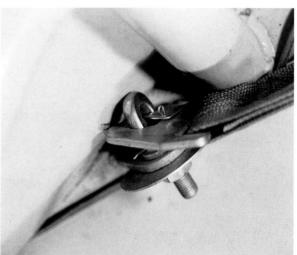

These three photos show mounting tabs for belts and harnesses. Use Grade 8 or better mounting hardware and tighten before every race. Make sure a cotter pin is used to keep the belt latch from coming out. In the photo on the bottom, the antisubmarine belt does not have a cotter pin in place. Use large washers to spread load and capture the belt hooks.

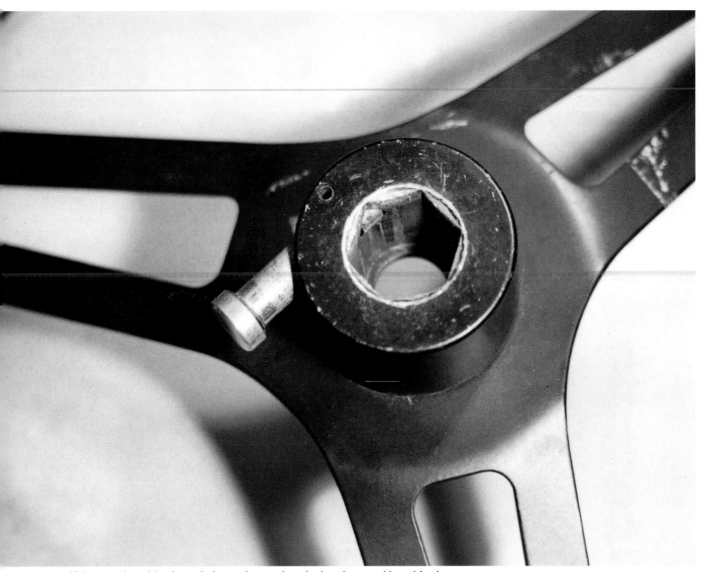

Make sure the quick-release device on the steering wheel works smoothly and freely.

Shear brackets should align so that the bolt shank is 90 degrees from the direction of pull. If brackets are off more than a couple of degrees, the bracket could bend under load, and bending could lead to failure.

A while ago, a friend was involved in a nasty crash. He spent a couple of weeks in the hospital with head injuries, a broken eye socket and other injuries. He's OK now, but he had a three-month recovery. The crash was a racing incident, but the injuries were completely avoidable. Being new to racing, this driver made one very serious mistake. While working on the vehicle, he removed the seat and the shoulder harness. In this vehicle, like many tube-framed late models, the shoulder har-

nesses bolt to a main chassis rail at floor level then pass around the back side of the lateral brace just below shoulder height. This allows the shoulder harness belts to pull against a cage tube at nearly a 90 degree angle to the spine and parallel to the direction of the force from a frontal impact. This holds the driver's upper body firmly in the seat and keeps it from moving too far forward in a crash. If the point of resistance on the harness is too far below the shoulder blades, the harness will allow the driver to move too far in a crash. In this case, the shoulder harness belts were *not* routed over the cage brace at shoulder height. Instead, the belts ran from the frame mount at floor level directly through the opening

The rod end holding the steering shaft should be cleaned and checked for tightness every race. Having the rod end come loose in a race could be dangerous.

Seat belt style window net releases contain plastic parts that can melt in a fire, making release more difficult. Spring-loaded and latch-link window net releases are the best.

in the back of the seat. Only the aluminum seat offered resistance to the force of a nearly head-on impact with the wall. The seat folded over, allowing the driver to reach as far forward as the windshield. The driver's movement bent the steering column, and his head in the area of the right eye socket hit the cage and fractured the skull bone around the eye. It was very serious stuff. Injuries would have been minimal had the shoulder harness belts been correctly routed over the cage cross-brace at shoulder level. *You need to be sure your belts are properly installed!*

Steering

The steering U-joint should be checked for free play every few races. Check the steering wheel mount bolts for tightness every few races. Clean and check the steering wheel quick-release mechanism every race.

Window Net

Make sure the window net is clean and tight. Clean the release mechanism every few races, more often if you race on dirt. If your window net release is an old seat belt release from a passenger car, be aware that the mechanism is made partially from plastic and can melt in a fire. Also, dirt and grit can get into the release and make exiting the car difficult in an emergency. It is best to use a latch-and-link style release or the slide-in, spring-loaded release, rather than a passenger car seat belt release.

These photos show the window net latch and bracket. Check the latch release every race for smooth operation. The window net needs to be kept clean, and it should be replaced every two to three years. The bracket should be checked every race for wear and cracks, especially around the welds.

Adhesive applied to rubber pedal pads assures they stay in place. It's dangerous and distracting to have one fall off in a race. Having your foot slip off the brake pedal while trying an outbraking pass is very annoying.

Good fire systems can save serious injury. Most pro-level racing requires them; smart racing demands them.

Dense roll bar padding can reduce injuries in a crash. Use only SFI Foundation approved padding. The padding should absorb energy and not rebound back to its original shape immediately.

Pedal Covers

If your pedals, especially the brake pedal, have a rubber cover, make sure that it is not damaged and is securely in place. If you use some other substance to improve traction on the pedals, make sure that it is working properly. This should be checked every event.

Roll Bar Padding

Roll bar padding also deteriorates with age, so it should be replaced every two to three years. If sections become torn, they provide reduced protection and should be replaced. Use zip-ties for installation, but point the joint of the zip-ties away from the driver.

Seat

Like the restraint belts, the seat must be bolted in properly and securely to be effective. Check mounting bolts for tightness routinely, at least every 10 to 12 events. Keep the upholstery clean. Grease and oil increase fire hazard greatly. Use warm water and a mild detergent or upholstery cleaner. Do not use any type of flammable solvent.

Fire Bottle

Fire bottles require little maintenance, but make sure the release cable works smoothly and is clean. This is especially important on dirt. Check the pressure gauge to be certain that the bottle is fully charged.

Crashes are an inevitable part of racing. Reducing the risk of injuries starts by using the best safety equipment properly installed. By taking the best care of your safety equipment, you will reduce the risk of injuries in crashes. Take the time to routinely check every piece of safety gear, and the results will be positive. Ignore safety equipment, and it will likely fail you at the exact moment you need it most.

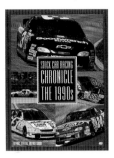

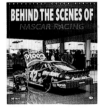
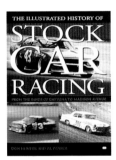

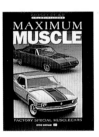